Gaining Altitude

Retirement and Beyond

Gaining Altitude

Retirement and Beyond

a memoir by
Rebecca Milliken

atmosphere press

Published by Atmosphere Press

Cover design by Beste Miray Doğan

atmospherepress.com

Table of Contents

Preface

Over the last ten years, since I turned 60, I have been somewhat unexpectedly immersed in what has seemed a deliberate process of change. I didn't intend to engage in such a process. But it has felt inevitable, necessary, and insistent. The centerpiece of this time of transformation has been the process of retirement—getting ready to contemplate the idea, dithering about whether or not it was *really* time to retire, and finally deciding to do it. Screwing up my courage, I dove off my familiar, time-worn, work-related cliff, leaving behind my life as a working stiff without the slightest idea of what would happen afterward.

Frankly, I am still amazed at what has unfolded. Before I turned sixty, I had never thought much about what retirement might look like nor about what I might do after, so every aspect of this time and experience has been a surprise. And it has been quite a journey. In the beginning, I rejected the idea out of hand and stayed in denial for a long while. I finally got feisty, braver, and honest with myself and let go. Freefall followed—a limbo, open time that was crucial to what came after. When I came up for air, I began to understand where I was headed and what I wanted to do and be, unearthing in myself as I did a profound desire to become a writer.

Along the way, as I moved toward a new life rhythm, I have had the privilege of conversations—far-ranging, open-ended, unexpected—with people who wanted to talk about retirement. Some wanted me to know they thought it was a stupid idea. Some wanted me to reassure them that there was life after retirement. Many wanted to tell me how rich and surprising their own experience with retirement had been and how much they were enjoying what had developed for them after they left the lives they had had before.

I wrote this book to tell my own story and to continue the conversation.

How did my retirement happen?
Once I was free, what came afterward?
What does this freedom hold?

Chapter One
Denial

"RETIRE??? Are you kidding? Why would I want to do that? I love my job!" I sputtered.

My retired friend Susan was visiting from out of town. She and I were having lunch at our favorite haunt—Bread and Chocolate on Connecticut Avenue—on a wet summer Wednesday afternoon in 2010. We had scuttled in from the teeming downpour, shaking out dripping umbrellas and leaving a trail of raindrops as we wove our way to the back table where we liked to sit. We settled into the bench seat, ordered our usual Caesar salad and coffee, and had gotten right down to what was a long-time habit of mutually musing about life.

The previous year, Susan, a fellow therapist who had been talking about retiring for a long time, finally did it. After thirty-five years of practicing as a psychotherapist, she decided it was time to find out what else she could do with her life. Over many months, she said goodbye to her clients, sold her office furniture, and finally closed the door of her practice. And then, much to my surprise, she announced that she and her husband were moving to Maine and leaving behind their old lives completely.

She told me about her new life in Maine, her new pursuits, the difference of having so much open time, her excitement over the changes, and what it felt like to be so free. And then she suggested it was time for me to think about retiring.

Hence my sputtering retort *"Retire??? Are you kidding?"* And I went on ... *"What would I do with myself?"*

"It isn't that I haven't struggled with all the unstructured time," she said as she stabbed at the leftover leaves of lettuce on her plate. "It just takes getting used to, and, once you do, there is finally time to do stuff you've never had time to do or never imagined doing."

I thought about this. What would it be like to have more time? Idly stirring my by-this-time cold coffee, I began to complain. "You are right that there never seems enough time, outside of work, to do stuff I want to do—like exercising or reading the newspaper or a good book. I never remember birthdays, and it's hard to find the time to plan a trip to someplace far away. I don't even visit my kids as often as I'd like." I stopped listing all the things I might do if I found the time. It was too depressing.

Her eyebrows knitted together as she fixed me with a serious look. She tapped the table with a knife. "You should be thinking about retiring *now!* It's time. There's so much more to life once you get done doing what you have always done."

She sat up straighter and gestured with her fork, her speech accelerating with enthusiasm. "Look at me! Look at all that's changed since I retired. I have a dog. I do yoga every day. I'm a lot more patient. I'm interested in stuff I haven't paid attention to in years. I'm learning more about classical music and how to change the oil in my car. I'm taking a class in proprioceptive writing—I didn't even know what that was before this! And I think I'm much more interesting, at least to myself." Breathless, she finished with a flourish of the fork for emphasis. "You really should try new stuff. It's great! But you *have* to retire first."

I could feel sweat bead on my forehead as my stomach lurched. Now that I thought about it, she *was* more interesting since she had retired. These days, she was always coming up with unfamiliar, new perspectives on life and following up by trying out things she hadn't considered before. But still, I just couldn't see myself doing what she was doing and actually retiring.

I'm happy in my work life, I reassured myself. *Why would I retire?* For the last thirty years, I had loved being a psychotherapist—helping people sort through the challenges and problems life threw at them. I had always been up for work-related discussion, seeking out new approaches, training groups, and new referrals. I was still healthy, and, freed up now that my kids had fledged, I could spend more time at work rather than less. This was my chance to enjoy what years of experience can give you—that sense of accomplishment and ease in knowing what you are doing.

Furthermore, I thought to myself, how can I stay in Washington D.C. and be *retired*? To people in this city, what you do for work is everything. Being retired in Washington meant being identity-less and is *not* looked on

7

as a happy, viable place to be. To be without a job, no matter how old you were, meant something terrible had happened. Susan had moved to Maine and didn't have to explain herself and what she was doing with her time the way I would have to in this work-obsessed, career-oriented city. The idea of giving up my hard-won professional life and identity didn't seem like even a remote possibility. Not a chance!

The very thought gave me the heebie-jeebies.

"I'm not ready to do that." I squirmed in my seat. "That would mean I would be designated 'over the hill,' done with, relegated to the sidelines." I waved my hand across the table as if to ward off the bad juju associated with the idea of retiring. "And, even if I did want to quit being a therapist, I haven't got a clue what else I would do if I gave up my job. I need to know what I'd do next before I make any changes."

Susan looked at me and rolled her eyes. "That's bullshit, you know. I learned that the hard way by waiting way too long to make the move. I wasted a lot of time trying to figure out what I was going to do after I retired. But you can't plan it out beforehand. You have to let go of what you were doing, of what you were, and be in limbo for a while before you can figure out what comes next."

Rapping the table harder than before and glaring at me, she said, "You have to *dismantle* stuff—let go of the job and the old routines, habits, ways of being. Empty out the space first, before you do anything else." She paused and looked at the middle distance beyond our table as if she were seeing into the future. Then, her gaze swiveled back at me.

"You are much more ready than you think."

I raised my chin and sat up straighter. "No, I'm not."

I was firm, decisive, sure.

"You'll see."

She knew me well.

And she was right. I just didn't want to admit it to anyone yet, including myself.

Chapter Two
Drift

Our family—my husband, two kids, and intermittent dogs, cats, rabbits, hamsters, turtles, and tropical fish—had lived for twenty years in a shambling stucco-and-clapboard house. It was perched on the edge of a ravine in which the majority of the raccoons in the District of Columbia resided. In the spring at night, the raccoons climbed to the tops of the trees that towered over our house and screeched—a mating ritual, I was told. A small creek sluiced through our backyard, creating a watery soundtrack we could hear from the back porch. When wading in the creek, we came upon purplish slugs clinging to the wet stones and wriggling crayfish in the sandy bottom. It was a little like living in the country in the middle of the city.

We moved to this house in 1991 when our two kids were just hitting their teenage years. Our house then was ground zero for frenetic activity and the accompanying dramas ... which in turn elicited a goodly measure of parental angsting as to whether we would all survive such tumultuous times. Not to mention the loud music, late-night homework crises, and the terrifying experiences of driving with a child who has just gotten his or her learner's permit—or, even worse, when that kid (by now a legal driver) is late getting home from a party to which you have reluctantly let him or her go.

There wasn't a lot of time or space to think deep thoughts or reflect much on the meaning or direction of our lives during that time. Like everyone else in this self-important town, we were all very, very busy. Our days were filled with to-ing and fro-ing from work and school and sports and appointments and everywhere else we had to go on any given day. Half-eaten bagels in hand, we scrambled out the door in the mornings—the four of us going in different directions all day long—and then landing back at home in the evening in time for more feverish activity and freighted exchanges about what had gone wrong or right in the day.

Back then, when I wasn't at work, there was always something that needed to be dealt with at home—who would drive my son to his hockey game on the Eastern shore, which required leaving at 5 AM on Saturday morning; whether my daughter could pierce her tongue; who had been smoking and *what* they were smoking in the cedar closet downstairs; what to do about the rescue dog we had adopted who had bitten the neighbor who climbed over our fence; whether someone could spend the night at a house where the parents were often away; what to have for dinner that we could all agree on, and so on. Endless. My husband and I were, in those years as parents, by turns, amused, perplexed, proud, horrified, relieved, overwhelmed, worried, and grateful. There was much to preoccupy us at home.

In comparison to life at home with teenagers, my professional life often seemed a refuge from the household commotion. I had been a practicing psychotherapist in D.C. and Maryland since 1982, had worked in public and private psychiatric hospitals, a homeless shelter, a jail, an Alzheimer's unit, and, finally, in my own private practice. Trained originally as an arts therapist, I used experiential, arts-based approaches (sand tray, dance-movement, and expressive arts therapy) as well as more traditional verbal approaches in my practice. I was lucky to teach and train with other professionals and enjoyed the rich collegial exchange that happened in trainings, supervision groups, and conferences. And, more recently, I was certified as an Imago couples counselor. This had brought new clients into my practice, and I was working hard to integrate this approach with these new arrivals.

Simply said, I loved my work. It grounded me.

Having a career—being able to work as well as have a family—has always been important to me. I graduated from college in 1972, just as the women's movement was taking hold. In contrast to the previous generation of women like me who often married, had children, and didn't work, I embraced the notion that I could do both. I was determined. So, my work in many ways shaped how and who I was in my world. It was, in large part, my identity. It counterbalanced my flip-side identity as mother, wife, and chief bottlewasher. Often, I even have to admit, it kept me sane in the face of the challenges of raising kids and helping them fledge—of getting them to a finish line, whatever that was going to be.

My kids eventually graduated from high school. First my son and then my daughter sailed off to college. They became twenty-somethings. Life at home was quieter and less worrying without the business of navigating teenage years with our children. Things seemed simpler if no less challenging in different ways. My twenty-something kids spent the next few years—as kids seem to do these days—moving in and out of the house, getting their future lives together. While they were doing this, my husband and I marshaled on with our lives—both of us still immersed in our work. Work continued to be sustaining for me. I was motivated and happy with my life the way it was. I didn't see the need to make any significant changes. The idea of retiring never even occurred to me during that time. Why would I do such a thing?

But that began to change. I began to change. The ground underneath my prescribed routines and way of doing life slowly but surely began to shift.

In the fall of 2010, I began to feel restless and distracted, both in and out of sessions. In my non-work hours, I took up some odd habits. On days when I wasn't seeing clients, I might change my clothes several times. Early in the day, I'd dress up as if going to work and sashay down to the kitchen to eat my oatmeal, feeling very professional and ready for action. But soon I'd feel itchy and uncomfortable and change into clogs and some stretched-out, baggy item leftover from my pregnant days. Later on, I might don tights, boots, and an orange sweater (a color I never wore but had in my closet for a time) and go out and walk the dog, pausing to gaze at my reflection as I passed windows of stores on Connecticut Avenue, wondering why I looked different to myself.

Nothing seemed to fit for long. I decided this must be a by-product of turning 60 that past spring. I told myself this was all part of figuring out what my new style was going to be now that I was into my seventh decade. But I didn't feel settled about this new tendency. I wondered why I felt the need to change my clothes so often. *Am I having some sort of identity crisis?* I quickly nixed that thought, denial being a familiar, knee-jerk reaction to uncomfortable possibilities I wasn't ready to deal with. *No way!* I reassured myself. *I'm experimenting, that's all. I'm just trying to figure out what fits the new 60-year-old me ... this is only about clothes.*

But my restlessness grew. Increasingly that fall, in my spare time, I would wander around the house—migrating from upstairs to kitchen to basement office and back again, depending on my mood. I had difficulty settling in for any length of time. One grey, wet Tuesday morning, I headed upstairs, determined to catch up on my reading. In a small bedroom on the top floor, I had piled the multiple un-read clinical journals and texts that I had brought home from my downtown office. I turned on Paul Winter's Wolf Eyes CD—mellow music would help me focus, right?—and tucked into the barcalounger we had stowed there. I reached for Susan Johnson's *The Practice of Emotionally Focused Couple Therapy* and dug in, comforted by the steady drumbeat of rain on the roof above my head. For a few minutes, I was absorbed— seduced by the idea that someone could tell me exactly what to do with those excruciatingly difficult moments in couple therapy sessions—but very quickly my focus gave way to a surging sleepiness, my eyelids getting heavy with the mesmerizing sound of rain as I slid lower in the barcalounger.

All I need is another cup of coffee, I thought. Springing out of the chair, I headed for the kitchen.

In the kitchen, I poured myself a fresh cup and stirred in half-and-half while I blankly stared out the window, not actually seeing what was there. I then felt the urge to pace around—out to the back porch to see how hard it was raining, then back to the kitchen to put away the half-and-half and turn off the coffee pot, then to the living room to plump up the pillows on the couch, and then back to the kitchen to wash my coffee cup—finally admitting to myself that I was feeling guilty about not getting any work done. With this in mind, I fled down to my office in the basement, determined to finish my notes on the last couple's session or fill out those unfinished insurance forms.

This behavior was, to say the least, unusual, if not downright disorienting, especially when I became unfocused and distracted while working. In sessions, my mind sometimes wandered. Occasionally—unreasonably, I thought—when I was seeing clients in my home office, I would get distracted, looking out the window at the weeds in the garden that needed to be pulled or fixate on how the picture hanging over my client's head needed straightening. Sometimes, in my downtown office, when a client was telling a long story, I would begin to think about what to have for dinner or who I needed to call after the session. I had to consciously yank my attention back to my client and remind myself to concentrate. Both in and out of sessions I often felt drifty and aimless—like a hamster on a wheel, in motion but not going anywhere in particular.

What was going on? My work had always grounded me in the past. Now I felt unsettled and I couldn't figure out why.

For a while, I tried to stave off this creeping sense of distraction and aimlessness. I made attempts to restore order and focus in my work life and bring renewed energy to my home life. I organized and filed away months' worth of client notes, artwork, and random articles, cleaned the oven and inventoried cans of food in our pantry that needed to be thrown away, signed up for a couples therapy workshop, re-applied myself to finishing client notes and overdue journal reading, and offered to host neighborhood Friday night porch parties.

One windy November afternoon, I even rearranged the living room furniture. I should have known that was a sign. When my husband got home from work that evening, he blew into the kitchen, where I was pouring myself a glass of wine. My husband is tall, fast-moving in the roadrunner sense, and energetic—the kind of guy who, at the end of a workday, flies in the door, ready for a cocktail and looking for something to talk about that has nothing to do with his work. As he pulled up onto a stool next to me, he leaned in, arched his left eyebrow, and peered down at me.

"I noticed that you rearranged the furniture in the living room."

In all the many years we had lived in this house, we had never, not once, rearranged the furniture in the living room.

"Interesting arrangement."

He paused.

"Didn't you like it the way it was?"

The answer was: not anymore. Change was coming. And I would eventually have to face that. Inexorably, I was drifting away from my old life.

Chapter Three
Change of Address

I had never imagined moving out of that house ... not really. But then, I'd never pictured myself as a 60-year-old, either.

But here I was, almost 61, not at all myself. I felt restless and discontent with the status quo ... the way things had been ... what was going on?

At the end of December 2010, my newly serious and suddenly professionally-coiffed daughter moved out of the room in which she had grown up—the one with faded yellow wallpaper and old yearbooks still in the closet—and out of our old, shambling house. I watched as she threw overstuffed suitcases and lumpy satchels filled with random tchotchkes, scarves, high heels, bulky necklaces, and running shoes into the back of her beat-up 1999 VW station wagon. She was moving to another city, with a new job, on her way to a new life.

As I saw her taillights disappear around the corner at the end of our street, I wondered what that would mean for her. I also could have asked myself then what this move would mean for my husband and me. But I didn't. Denial is a steadfast habit where I am concerned. I wasn't ready yet to admit to myself that her move would presage a new life for us as well.

A month later, on an icy, leaden January Saturday, my husband suggested that we spend the morning going to open houses—looking at apartments.

"'Just for the fun of it. It'll be like doing calisthenics," he said.

"And why would we be doing calisthenics?"

I was wary.

"You know. You do calisthenics to develop stamina, strength, and flexibility ... fitness with a capital F."

"Fitness for what?" As if I didn't know.

He looked at me quizzically to see if I was seriously asking.

My husband sometimes looks just like Mark Twain—thick, white hair akimbo, blue eyes ready to suss out the ironies of life, and a bushy, untrimmed mustache that covers a small smile whenever he poses an irreverent question. As was his habit when pointing out what he thought was obvious, he cocked his head, gave me a hard stare, and continued.

"Fitness for the future. Building new muscles for ..." He paused, waiting for me to fill in the blank. When I didn't, he went on: " ... for whatever is going to happen in the future."

My husband had been talking about moving into an apartment for years. In fact, throughout our marriage, he was known to become wildly and unaccountably enthusiastic about moving anywhere—just for the novelty.

Often, when we were driving north from Washington to New England, just before we'd enter the tunnel in Baltimore, he'd suggest we move to that city.

"MICA is a fantastic art school! Let's look for an apartment within walking distance to it."

He'd look my way, anticipating excited agreement.

For a minute, I'd take the bait. "Who in this family has time to go to art school? And why Baltimore?" Then I would go back to listening to NPR to show him I was not willing to engage in this gambit.

He'd be crestfallen until we got to Wilmington.

So on this particular morning, I decided to treat this apartment-looking with a grain of salt, just a diversionary outing to humor my imaginative mate. And anyway, I told myself, given our history of glacial decision-making, nothing was going to happen quickly. Famous last words.

During this 'casual' apartment-looking tour, we came upon one that was so undeniably different from anything we had lived in before that it felt a little like we were visiting an exotic foreign country. What made it so different for us was that it had been recently renovated, and thus everything in this apartment was apparently working and relatively new. There was no peeling paint, and no running toilets or leaky gutters. It was in a part of town inhabited by much younger people and offered— according to the agent stationed in the lobby—infinite "walkability." (This last term had to be explained to me.) And the kitchen, unlike all our larger previous kitchens, was the size of a peanut—efficient, modern, neat, and tiny.

Like most city apartments, it had no direct access to the outdoors.

"There's no front and backyard to tend!" my husband

crowed as he sailed by me in search of the circuit board and fuse box, in earnest dialogue with the agent.

"It certainly isn't what we are used to," I commented as I wandered down the long, well-lit hallway that ran the length of the apartment. Nothing in our old house could be described as well-lit due to antiquated electrical wiring. "The washing machine is right around the corner from the bedroom. Everything is on the same floor!"

"Exactly," said my husband as he rounded the corner and sped back in my direction. He was practically levitating with excitement; his six-foot frame bobbing up and down as he approached me. Skidding to a stop and gesticulating energetically, he almost shouted. "It's perfect. No more schlepping things up and down stairs. No more worrying about what's happening in the basement when you're on the third floor. No more broken furnaces, no more wondering if the cracks in the walls are because the house is settling or something else!"

I listened nervously as he enumerated the rest of the "no-mores" he could think of. I thought to myself, *Perfect? Really? For us?*

But then I began to reconsider. *What was perfect for us these days, now that the kids had moved out and on? Maybe we were ready for a real change? Why not?*

This feeling was a little like having a spell cast on us. Or being caught up in some sort of alien gravitational force field pulling us away from familiar territory. It wasn't rational. But we were hooked.

Three weeks later, we put a bid in on the apartment. Buying an apartment at this time—especially buying one so rapidly—had not been our plan. Not even, he confessed later, my husband's secret plan. At least it hadn't been obvious to us that we had set out that day with this objective in mind. We certainly had never admitted out loud that we were ready to make this colossal change in our lifestyle.

It was shocking to us and, at the same time, shockingly easy—finances aside, that is. How could we explain this to ourselves?

As we walked out of the bank after deciding to put in our bid, I looked sideways at him. "What are we thinking? Are we nuts? We haven't even begun to think about selling our house."

He nodded slowly. "Yup. Out of our minds."

I have always been intrigued by the idea of tipping points. A tipping point, according to the Merriam-Webster dictionary, is "the critical point in a situation, process or system beyond which a significant and often unstoppable effect or change takes place." Alternatively, it is described on Whatis.com as "a point in an evolving situation that leads to new and irreversible development." In other words, tipping points often lead to major life transitions.

I knew a lot about transitions. I spent my career studying the process of transition and working with people who were trying to navigate change in their lives. Looking for tipping points was a primary focus in my work—helping people get to this kind of an edge, a threshold over which they could step into newness. It usually took much longer than people wanted it to take. On the way, we often, together, became impatient, unable to see progress or signs that anything was changing.

Again and again, I'd have to remind myself and my clients of the fact that change is a process, not a singular event or phenomenon, and is often taking shape below the surface before it becomes visible. It evolves. Life goes on as it has before; situations, behaviors, habits, and routines continue while, behind the scenes, in some subterranean place in the psyche, the sands are shifting; something is germinating. Finally, things add up, and a seemingly small event, circumstance, or situation presents itself—and that becomes the catalyst for real change.

And then, surprise, surprise, the change that happens is often startling—somehow unexpected, not anticipated or imagined when it was just an abstraction. The teeter-totter has become unbalanced and tipped over into something entirely new.

Clearly, my husband and I had reached a tipping point. We were finally ready for something new and suddenly able to act to make it happen. But what had got us there? What was the tipping point? And why were we so surprised?

As I reflect on our life then, I see how our situation had been evolving over the previous years—how many factors played into this shift, like a series of dominoes leaning on one another until the last one makes the whole deck fall over. In the years before we decided to move, we had experienced many changes. In my case, my grandmother— 108 years old—had died five years earlier. This was a monumental, if not much-anticipated, event. My father at 92 followed suit three years later, a milestone that was also anticipated but immensely sad for me. (My mother had died many years before.) I was then officially an orphan, no longer anyone's daughter or granddaughter, while also now a member of the oldest generation in my shrinking family. That felt significantly different. A new vantage point from which to view the world.

Loss creates openings whether we welcome them or not. My particular losses offered me the opportunity to step away from the roles I had always taken—the rule-follower, the purposeful worker bee, the good citizen. I felt a new kind of freedom; I no longer had to operate according to old templates and expectations. I felt newly feisty and ready to find out what else was possible for me. I hadn't anticipated this shift in my sense of self, and it took a while to register what it would mean for me. Who was I going to be if I was no longer the person I had been used to being in my family?

On the other hand, my husband was having a different family experience. His parents were still very much alive and lived in a faraway state. With his parents and other relatives growing older, there were new responsibilities to be taken on. His role as an important member of his family was, if possible, getting larger. He had also taken on leadership roles in community organizations outside of work that required new energy and commitments, so he was spending more time away from home. He was spread too thin and needed more space and time to follow up on these new obligations. I hadn't realized how ready he was for a change, and, in particular, how ready he was to jettison the role and responsibilities of worrying about our old house.

I can't claim now that we were consciously thinking and talking about all of this during the fall of 2010 before our daughter moved out. But by the time she moved, we had reached the tipping point. The house felt like an old shoe, one we had worn comfortably for twenty years. It had served us well and contoured to the needs and desires of our family life back then. But it just didn't fit anymore. It had gotten worn down, misshapen, too stretched out for us. It was too big. It represented our old life. It was time to make a change and create a new home.

Six months later, we said goodbye to the old house that I had loved for housing our family so well during all that frenetic activity, teenage drama, work challenges, and important milestones. Even our now-grown-up children supported our move. They were busily building new lives for themselves in New York and Oregon. They weren't worried about having a place to sleep in our new abode, nor were they feeling sentimental about our old house. So, without looking back and with no regrets, we packed up and moved into the apartment.

A day in the life of our new apartment meant waking up to the possibility of doing even the smallest activity in a different way than we had done it before. Surprising us randomly. Freeing.

Without thinking consciously about what we were doing, we developed new routines and habits. We woke earlier in the morning. The light and the birds outside our bedroom window woke us often long before 7 AM, so we had time before work to read for an hour. We never ate in the apartment kitchen or even in the dining room much—choosing instead to have picnics on our bed or in the hidden back room with the fireplace, where we ate on our laps or on a card table. We seldom cooked in that compact kitchen; tuna fish, salami, and salad were common fare. And, on a daily basis, we took great satisfaction in how many fewer books, pots, pans, pets, old vases, winter coats, porch chairs, and unmatched bathroom towels we owned and had to put away.

Practically everything that was required for daily living was within walking distance, and yet our world became more international. At the dry cleaners, we heard about life in Mongolia from the grinning, voluble woman who had just arrived in DC and who always wore red or orange. We frequented a crowded, Italian coffee shop where we could have cucumber gelato with our morning coffee. On the way to the subway, we'd pass embassy neighbors speaking French, Portuguese, and other languages I didn't recognize. There was a farmer's market on Sundays, a bookstore that doubled as a bar, a sandwich shop, and a postage-stamp-sized park where I could sit in the shade on a bench and watch other people's dogs run after tennis balls ... and be glad I was no longer a dog owner.

"How do you like living in an apartment? Do you miss the house?" friends asked.

My husband would gleefully hold up the key to the front door in answer. "Here's the only tool I need nowadays. No more rakes, shovels, hammers, leaf blowers, spades, lawnmowers, and, best of all—no more weeds!"

"Where do we keep the toilet paper?" I would ask every time I needed another roll.

"I haven't the vaguest idea," he'd answer. For months we didn't know where anything was. For some reason this was liberation.

"Talk about change," my husband said as we ambled slowly up the hill from the farmer's market in Dupont Circle to our apartment on a sunny Sunday afternoon. "Since we moved out of the old house, nothing is the same.

We don't even seem like the same people. Whoever thought it would be so easy to give up the life we had there?" He took another bite of the Honeycrisp apple he had just bought and chewed. "What do you think we will give up next?"

That was the sixty-four thousand dollar question, wasn't it? I thought. Now we had gotten the ball rolling, who knew what would come next?

Chapter Four
A Reckoning

I was surprised by all the change that happened as a result of moving to the apartment. I hadn't anticipated that so many of my old routines, habits, and familiar ways of doing daily life would change so quickly and effortlessly—that it would be so easy to adapt to our new living arrangements. I relished the newness and differences I was experiencing and frankly hoped that the restlessness I had been feeling over the last year would subside as a result of our move.

But, much to my chagrin, it didn't. In fact, if anything, I was more restless and at times even impatient during working hours. It was as if—now that I had experienced so much unexpected pleasure in the unfamiliarity and openness of my non-working hours—I felt an urge to bring the same sense of liberation and difference into the rest of my waking hours. But I still wasn't ready to admit to myself or anyone else that the urge translated into readiness for retirement. NO WAY!

Despite my determination to hold my course, over the next many months, in moments at work, during therapy sessions, I found myself distracted, disengaging from what people were talking about, unplugged. At those times, I would suddenly snap back to attention ... scolding myself for having lost the thread. I was restive during some of these hours, champing at the bit for the session to be over so I could feel free. I wasn't sure what I wanted to be free to do, but in these moments an urge to escape from my familiar routine would shoot through me, and I would have trouble sitting still.

What was happening? My therapy life didn't feel particularly stale or broken. I was not yearning for an end to a 'working life' or desperate for more leisure time. At the same time, I had to admit to myself that I sometimes felt that I just didn't want to be so responsible, so dutiful, so present as was necessary as an actively practicing therapist. I felt less and less willing to give myself over to those hours of focused listening and reflection.

Then one day something happened in a session that gave me significant pause and made me sit up and take notice.

It was my first appointment on a blustery Thursday morning in late January. It was spitting snow outside the window, and the old-fashioned radiators in my office were hissing as the heat rose. I poured myself a cup of coffee from my thermos, set it on the side table, and opened the door for the couple I had not met before who I had heard talking loudly and thumping around in the waiting room.

The wife stalked into the room and sat down hard in the chair across from me. Her husband, more tentative, hunched, followed and sat.

It seemed she didn't need an invitation from me to start talking. Eyes wide and bleary, waving her arms first up, then out and around her head, she began to yell at her husband. As she did, her carrot-red bangs fell into her face.

"Really?" she shrieked. "What was it that possessed you to put pictures of your mistress on your Facebook page? And what about the Paris trip you two took that you charged on our joint American Express account? Did you really think I wouldn't notice? And now you say that because you are willing to come to a couples therapist, I should forgive you and take you back? Are you fucking kidding me?" She punctuated the last question with a wild pivot of her intense glare from him to me and back to him.

Her husband, frozen statue-like, sat across the room, staring out the window. He didn't answer. Deadpan expression.

"Really???" she said again—this time with more volume. Red-faced, she whirled toward me with an infuriated grimace and said, "You're a couples therapist, right? What are YOU going to do about this? About him? Fix him. Fix this!"

I had been in this situation before. Many people come to therapy to be 'fixed' or, even more often, to get their partner 'fixed.' In situations like this, one partner may be so overwhelmed with raw emotion that they haven't had a chance to express or even get in touch with until they come to therapy, and then it bursts out. Sometimes the emotion is hurt—sometimes it is anger or intolerable despair. This wife was beyond furious and needed to let it out. Entering my office was her opportunity to say what had been festering inside her for weeks. She felt entitled to this moment and to her fury and sense of betrayal and hurt. And perhaps she was. This situation wasn't unusual for a couples therapy session. What *was* unusual was my reaction.

I paused for a long moment after she had finished her outburst. I could feel my face flush. I knew from long experience that this was nervousness about feeling something I shouldn't be feeling. In fact, I felt more like a coiled rattlesnake ready to strike than a calm, compassionate couples therapist. I was afraid I might leap up and muzzle this woman. I didn't feel ready to calm her nor to help them connect or even speak to each other. Instead, I wanted to put my fingers in my ears and tell this wife to just stop yelling so that I could suggest that maybe they ought to take these problems somewhere else. In that moment I didn't want to fix him or this situation or anything at all.

What in the world is the matter with me? I asked myself as I shifted around and re-crossed my legs in hopes of calming myself and staving off the rush of impatience. *What's going on? I'm supposed to try and help these people sort out their problems and instead all I want is for them to leave my office so I can do something else. Yikes!*

Thankfully, after a few seconds, I got ahold of myself. My impatience ebbed, my heart slowed a notch, and my therapist self re-emerged. Summoning my better instincts, I leaned toward this very upset woman and said, as gently as I could, " I am so sorry that you are in so much pain. I can sure see how it is you would feel hurt, angry, and exposed by what you discovered about your husband's infidelity. I wonder what, in this moment, you might need to help you feel calmer and more supported so that you can tell your husband how it has felt to be betrayed in these ways. And I am going to give you a minute to think that through while I say something to your husband."

I turned to him, paused again to take a breath, and then said, "It seems like you guys are in quite a pickle of a situation. But your wife mentioned you were willing to come into couples therapy, and I imagine that means you are willing to listen to what she has to say. She needs a good listener right now. Could you do that now, knowing there will be a chance for you to be heard as well in the future?"

That's what a compassionate, steadying therapist is supposed to say when a new client comes in as upset as this woman was. I was immensely relieved that I had steadied myself and was able to say it. The good news is that we all calmed down that day, and that these people were so absorbed in their own misery that they didn't seem to notice my impatience if it showed. I sure hope it didn't, though I am not claiming that this was a great therapy moment.

I must clarify something here. The feelings I describe having that day weren't about these people or their particular situation. It wasn't that this woman was impossible or unlikeable, or that there was no way to work with the anger and hurt in that room that day. This was about me. These unsettling, edgy reactions I was experiencing were smoke signals from a part of my brain I wasn't paying enough attention to then. I realized I had some reckoning to do with myself.

After they left, I sank back into my chair, exhausted. I thought back to the conversation with Susan, my friend from Maine, when she had told me I was more ready than I knew to retire. *Am I ready to retire, at last?* I wondered.

Can I finally admit this to myself? The thought still shocked me.

It took a couple of months and more of those disquieting, difficult therapy moments to bring home to my stubborn psyche the fact that I was much more ready than I was admitting. I wanted to be free. It was getting to be time.

Chapter Five
Letting Go

Just because I had this inner urge to be free, and it seemed that retirement was the inevitable next step, the path forward was not at all clear. I certainly didn't have a plan for how this new phase would go, and frankly, I still had recurring doubts as to the timing or whether it was even what I wanted or needed to do at this point.

I don't like endings, so I often avoid them. I'm not sure why. I usually leave sporting events and concerts before they are finished, much to my husband's chagrin. I am the first out of any class, workshop, birthday party, or gathering, often without having said goodbye. On the other hand, I sometimes resist leaving even when it's past time for me to go. It took me two and a half years to leave my first internship even though officially I was only supposed to be there a year. And, after ten years of working in a psychiatric hospital, I knew it was time to go, but spent the next several months quitting and then un-quitting.

More importantly, I had been working since I got out of college and had, for all those years, organized my life and my family's life around my husband's and my work schedules. Did I want to give that up? *Could* I give it up?

I dithered, nervous at the thought of giving up so much. Every time I forced myself to try and picture what this would look like, my chest would tighten and my heart would begin to thud. As I trudged up the steep hill home after a day at the office, as I wandered the aisles of the grocery store, as I microwaved my cold coffee for the third time—having forgotten to drink it the first and second time—questions somersaulted around in my head ... *how does one go about letting go of all of this?*

Sometimes, between client hours in my downtown office, sitting in my therapy chair, I would stare as if in a trance at the many dog-eared books and journals in the bookcases, reflecting on all that I had studied and tried in my practice. Looking at the titles felt like a bittersweet walk down memory lane; *The Family Crucible, Codependent No More, The Arts in Psychotherapy, After The Affair*. My body went very still in these moments. My muscles braced as I held back an ocean of hard feelings— fear and loss.

To avoid such thoughts and feelings at the end of the day, I would scramble out of my hard-to-get-out-of, low-slung chair, hurriedly sweep up my files, book bag, and coat, and fly out the door, in motion and relieved. One day I gamely rounded the corner in the dim hallway outside my office, attempting to catch the elevator before the doors shut, and crashed headlong into Eddie, the long-suffering and wise keeper of our office building. Eddie was the building superintendent. He was the guy who not only took care of the building but often me as well—helping me hang pictures and put together furniture when I first moved in, overseeing my entrances and exits mornings and evenings. Always there, brown shirt and khakis, raft of keys attached to his belt, a fixture of life at the office—steady, calm, good-natured.

"You in some sort of hurry to leave?" he asked, chuckling as he helped me pick up the items strewn about from the collision.

"Not at all," I said, brushing off the drops of diet coke that had spilled on my slacks from the half-drunk can I had been clutching. I tried to look dignified as I gathered my stuff and pushed the button for the elevator. I smiled brightly at him, waved goodbye, and dove into the elevator.

As the elevator made its slow, creaky way to the ground floor, I stared at the old-fashioned brass gridwork on the door that Eddie polished every week and pondered his question.

Why exactly was I in a hurry to leave that evening?

I was hurrying, I had to admit, to get away from feeling what I was feeling in the office. I was hurrying away from the realization that something so big, so important in my life was coming to an end.

At such moments, I doubted myself and this urge to be free. I would revert to thinking that the idea of ending my career seemed illogical, if not ridiculous. Why *would* I stop doing what I had poured so much time and energy into for so many years?

What was it I had loved about this work that so many people thought was just talking about pain, problems, and pitiable situations? The answer to that question—for me—

was that there was much to love ... and it had not been all pain, problems, and pitiable situations by any stretch.

For one thing, I hadn't always been just a talk therapist. I had started my career as a dance/movement therapist—a kind of arts therapist who works with movement and non-verbal expression as well as words. This approach invites the body into the conversation to release tension, to break through resistance, to encourage connection to self and others through active movement, creative expression, and the opportunity to be part of a unique group experience that doesn't insist on verbal disclosure. It is a playful medium through which people can let loose a little without losing control and find their way to a feeling without needing words.

In my groups at the hospital where I had worked for ten years, I loved watching as adolescent, shaggy-haired boys with ratty, baggy jeans got a chance to stomp around the room instead of having to talk about how angry they felt. Afterward, they'd collapse onto the floor in mock exhaustion, complaining about how tiring it had been to spend all that time stomping around, and then maybe make the connection to how tiring it was to be that angry.

And I loved seeing women in an addictions group, wound so tight they looked like they weren't breathing, allowing themselves to slowly unwind, begin to sway in time with the music and allow themselves to stretch out, expand, and eventually reach out. To watch the surprise and pleasure on so many of their faces as they relaxed, became part of the group, and took risks they hadn't thought possible was often deeply moving. Trust falls were always the most powerful—practicing falling and being caught—an unfamiliar sensation for most with issues of trust and control. Movement metaphor ... you can't beat it.

This approach served me well when I later became a more conventional talk therapist. It taught me to pay attention to non-verbal expressions—that stiffened, straight up-and-down posture of a spouse on the couple's first visit to therapy, the intense, shifting eye contact of a newly-sober person, the hidden horror reflected in the way a client who feels cornered huddles in her chair. Even as I paid attention to what was being said during sessions, sometimes non-verbal cues were what helped me understand better what was actually going on or not being said aloud.

Hearing people's stories—strange or confusing or tragic or frightening or inspiring or even funny—that's what talk therapy is all about. I loved helping people sort through the challenges and problems life threw at them: the mother whose teenage daughter was suicidal, the couple struggling after her in-laws had moved in with them, a young woman dealing with bulimia, a priest about to leave the church. I celebrated with them when they felt better, and stayed with them and their confusion and disappointment when they didn't, exploring how they might change their circumstances and if not, why not. Change is not easy. But working with so many different people who were willing to be so open about their struggles helped me become vastly more empathic.

It was a privilege and a huge responsibility to be trusted in this way. I learned as much—if not more—from my clients as we muddled through their issues together as they learned from me. Every day I got to see some version of courage or resilience and was always moved by the unyielding drive in so many to understand who they were and why they made the choices they did.

That was what I loved about being a therapist.

So why would I want to give this up?

That was the resounding question I heard from all sides once I floated my idea with friends and family.

"Why in the world would you want to stop working now?" queried my lawyer friend, Mary, who loved her job at AID and frequently traveled to places like Abu Dhabi and Sierra Leone. She wrinkled her face as if she smelled something bad. "You enjoy your work. You worked hard to get to where you are. And no one in D.C. retires voluntarily. How will you explain yourself?"

"What are you going to do all day long?" asked Kate, the landscape architect who worked all week and then wrote books about her work on weekends. She had a bewildered tone in her voice. "Play bridge? Take up golf?" Then, with a searching, somewhat sorrowful look at me, she said, "And what will you tell people at parties when they ask you what you are, what you do?" This she offered almost as a rhetorical question, the assumption being that there is no answer to who and what you are once you have retired.

Fellow therapists wondered how and why I would give it all up. "You love your job! Why would you want to retire? Why not just work fewer hours if you are burnt out?" These were people with whom I'd spent years in conversations about all the issues and conundrums we faced as therapists. I knew I would miss these conversations. And even more worrying—what would I talk about when I was no longer working? At this point, I had no idea.

Finally, many of the colleagues I consulted finished the

conversations with a stern admonishment: "If you don't know what else you want to do, why would you stop? Keep working until you have a plan!"

Frankly, during these conversations, I was embarrassed—feeling out of step with the world I had inhabited for the last many years and unable to fully explain myself. It wasn't that I was tired of working or burnt out. Even though I didn't have a clue as to what I would do afterward, I just knew that I didn't *want* to do what I had been doing anymore.

It was as if a friendly but feisty, *very determined* gremlin had taken up residence inside me, whispering in my ear regularly, insisting that I upend my work life as I had known it and get on with whatever would come next. More and more, I didn't feel in control of the momentum toward change. The gremlin seemed to be getting the upper hand, urging me forward even as I wondered where this would all lead. Needless to say, this was deeply unsettling and at times bewildering.

The closer I got to following through and making a date to retire, however, the louder another voice in my head started in. This voice was cautionary, disapproving, clear in its don't-do-this message. *If you retire, what are you going to do to help the world? You can't just retire and not do anything worthwhile!* And then this bothersome voice would up the ante. *You should do more, not less, with your time now that you don't have to worry about aging parents and children. You're at the top of your game. Use all that experience to do something really big, make a difference!* I was at war with myself—the gremlin— grinning ear to ear as if enjoying the battle with the stiff, brow-furrowed, black-hatted Puritan—self-righteous and guilt-inducing.

After nights of tossing and turning, I would argue with the stern don't-do-this voice while I brushed my teeth in the morning. Shaking my toothbrush defiantly at my disheveled reflection in the mirror, I would try to reassure myself. "It's okay not to have a career anymore! I've paid my dues. I get to do this now that I am this old." Then I would throw on my work clothes and clump into the kitchen where my husband would be innocently eating his yogurt and granola, watching ESPN. Feeling grumpy, I was impatient with everything.

"Why are you watching ESPN at 8 in the morning?"

He watched ESPN any chance he got when I wasn't around. I stabbed at the buttons on the remote. "Can't we turn on the weather channel? And why do the guy broadcasters keep interrupting that woman announcer with bad football jokes?"

On mornings like this, my husband knew better than to try and answer my cantankerous questions. He knew I was trying to get ready to retire, and since he couldn't yet imagine it for himself, he understood that it wasn't an easy decision. He'd quietly watch as I whirled around our minuscule kitchen, grabbing items for my lunch and dumping them into my recycled cloth grocery bag while microwaving the coffee that had gotten cold and muttering about not knowing what the weather was outside or what coat to wear to work. As I'd head for the door, still muttering, he'd poke his head out of the kitchen, say goodbye, and—somewhat ironically—wish me luck for the day.

I was frequently disoriented and caught up in my head, not paying attention. I would be driving down Connecticut

Avenue to a dentist appointment or to CVS, places I had been going to for thirty-plus years, and end up in Maryland before I noticed I had gone too far. I had trouble making even small, ridiculous decisions—like whether to buy cheddar or swiss cheese at the market, and then come home with provolone—a cheese neither of us liked.

I had to admit I was worried about what I would do with myself after I retired. I ruminated on possibilities. Would I decide to learn Arabic? Volunteer for the Red Cross? Take up pickleball? Go back to work as something else? Write a book about retirement? Become more domestic and start to cook? Maybe I should go to graduate school, but in what?

But the question was not what I would do after I retired. The real question for me at this point was: could I de-construct this work identity without falling apart? Or would I go into free fall and feel worthless, invisible, lost?

I dreaded feeling useless, boring, bored, and without focus. Could I avoid this by deciding now what I would do afterward?

At some point, I remembered Susan, the friend who had moved to Maine, saying that she had wasted a lot of time trying to figure out beforehand what to do after she retired.

"You can't plan it out beforehand. You have to let go of what you were doing, of what you were, and be in limbo for a while before you can figure out what comes next."

One late afternoon in the winter of 2012, I was sitting in my office sipping lukewarm lemonade I had bought at lunchtime and staring out the window. I watched pigeons swoop in, line up like sentinels on the roof of the building across from my office, and fluff up against the cold. I was not thinking about anything in particular ... just feeling restless, impatient with having to see three more clients before I could go home. *Why,* I wondered, *did my office feel suddenly like a closet—claustrophobic, lacking in fresh air?* I suddenly wanted to bolt— to get up and get out and escape the steam heat and mauve and puce-colored walls that were closing in on me.

I didn't run away from my office that afternoon. Instead, I took a long, hard look at myself. For too long I had been making excuses for waiting just a bit longer, waiting perhaps for some kind of sign, resistant to making a final decision to retire but growing edgier and edgier around work responsibilities. I felt at last truly impatient with myself and my dithering. *What in the world am I waiting for? If not now, when?*

There it was. It suddenly seemed so clear. I was not only ready but itching to set myself free, to pry my clenched fingers off of that hard-won professional identity, to let go of what had defined me and step out into something else, as yet unknown. I didn't care what. I just knew I needed to turn the corner and find my way to a new way of doing life.

It was like stepping over that edge you had been looking at for a long time—out into open air and nothingness.

I set a date and began the process of closing my practice. This took months. I had seen many clients off and on for years. It felt inconceivable that I would never again see these people I knew so well and, conversely, that I was truly not going to be there for them anymore. How could I not be there to support the young man who had been rejected by his evangelical parents for being gay? Or to help the recently widowed mother who now had to figure out how to manage children and step-children and her future life on her own?

"What do you mean you are retiring?" asked one client. "You aren't old enough to retire. Are you sick?"

Another was furious. I had always assured her, she said, that I would be there if she wanted to come back into therapy. Now I was changing the contract. I was taking myself out of the game, beyond her reach, out of service. It wasn't fair.

I had to agree. "You are right. I am changing the contract. I won't be here anymore. And you are also right that it doesn't seem fair." I hated having to face the fact that I was letting people down, reneging on what had seemed like a promise, something I never wanted to do and had thought I would never do. But this was definitely part of the process—facing up to the disappointment and disillusion that some clients felt.

Others accepted my retirement with equanimity and as an opportunity to move on. All of them, though, knew it meant ultimately saying goodbye for good.

It was such a monumental change. It was so final. But I was determined and sure at last, as sad and nervous as it sometimes made me.

As it turned out it was that—the finality—that made these endings in the end so much less difficult than I had imagined. This was It. And once I truly acknowledged that finality, I felt a clarity and calm I had rarely experienced in other major life transitions. It was as if a dense fog had lifted, offering a longer view of things, and I could finally see straight. Despite the doubting voice that continued to echo in my head, the momentum to move on and out and the clarity that this was the right decision was stronger.

Not all the endings were happy or good, but they happened nonetheless. My clients and I had the chance to say what is often left unspoken and then to really say goodbye in the months that followed. I was able to say to my clients how much the work had meant to me, how much I was going to miss it and them. And, in turn, the finality and sense of calm allowed my clients to openly express their sadness or anger when they felt it, or their fears for the future, or even their relief that our work was done. What else could we ask for in ending something meaningful?

Years before, I had been seeing a couple as they struggled with issues in their marriage and with their adopted son. I had grown quite fond of them and was shocked to learn in an evening session during their second year of therapy that the husband had been diagnosed with pancreatic cancer. They came into the office for a few more months but eventually he could no longer leave his house. Therapy was out of the question.

The last time I saw him was when I visited them at home to say goodbye. When I arrived, this gentleman was waiting, wrapped in a soft, faded blue bathrobe, sitting quietly on the couch in his living room. He peered up at me as I walked in, a grin slowly spreading over his ashen face, and asked if I had received his change of address postcard yet? Puzzled, I looked over at his wife. She shook her head slowly and said, "Lenny wanted to be sure you knew he is already on his way to someplace new. He's almost there." He died two weeks later.

I was profoundly saddened by this lovely man's death and afterward thought much about my last visit to this couple. There was something infinitely peaceful about this goodbye—as final as it was. Finality gives us a sense of closure for sure.

Maybe ending my work as a therapist was a kind of death. Perhaps death is required. This may be the only way we make room for something entirely new. As I was going through the process of retiring, I didn't think about it that way, but now, as I look back, I can see that it was a kind of death. I should have known that final goodbyes have their own special essence ... clarity and inescapable doneness.

Dismantling my professional life meant finally acknowledging that I was really done with being a therapist. This identity had defined me and shaped the way I had been in the world for many years. But it no longer fit who I was becoming. I needed to clear the space for whatever would come next by letting it go, giving it up. You can't move on until you finish doing what you were doing. That's what I learned. That's what I did.

"All changes, even the most longed for, have their melancholy; for what we leave behind us is part of ourselves; we must die to one life before we can enter another."

Anatole France

"What we call the beginning is often the end
And to make an end is to make a beginning.
The end is where we start from."

T.S. Eliot

"Little Gidding"

Chapter Six
Free Fall

I was lucky. Once I had taken the leap, emptied my office, and officially retired, I could run away from my life temporarily—or, to be more specific, from the life where work happened.

It seemed the logical thing to do ... to leave behind the routines and schedules, the responsibilities and obligations, the familiarity of my busy, hurrying, concentrating, head-down working life and go to a different kind of space ... to sort of disappear on my old self and my way of being in the world.

And as it happens, this is exactly what the experts (transition specialists, cultural historians, elders in traditional and ancient cultures, and authors who write about change) recommend—a hiatus between one life and another—a departure from what was. These experts propose that people who are navigating a major personal or professional change in life take some time after an ending and, if possible, vacate their familiar circumstances, at least for a while. You need, according to these experts, to literally get lost for a time—"lost enough," as Robert Frost said in his poem *Directive,* "to find yourself."

Some people, like author Cheryl Strayed, decide to walk the Pacific Crest Trail alone after her mother's death and her own divorce. Others drop out and go live on the beach in Mexico, as a lawyer friend did after years as a public defender. My husband's uncle went to Australia for six months after being fired from his job by his brother-in-law. Other people go on silent retreats or yoga workshops or stay at home and find time to be quiet and alone. There are all sorts of ways to get away. Bottom line, it seems some sort of retreat—in both senses of the word—is what the doctor orders for this kind of time after a significant ending or life change.

So getting out of town was a good idea.

It was May of 2012 when I saw my last client. The next week, Eddie, my superintendent friend, jingling his keys and editorializing on the best way to lift heavy items without hurting your back, helped my husband and I move the furniture out of my office. It didn't take long to dismantle the space. Surprising myself, I felt no pangs as we lifted and shoved everything into the padded elevator. Thirty years of accumulated therapy office accouterments—done with. I kept the two Ikea chairs I had put together when I moved to this downtown office in 2000, and sent the rest (bookcases, file cabinets, desk, desk chair, and several framed pictures of bucolic landscapes meant to calm the agitated spirits of clients) to Goodwill. It felt as if I was handing over the coin of the realm, turning in my keys. My lease expired at the end of the month.

A week later, I left town. I went to Maine and moved into a middle space between who I had been and who I might become.

My husband and I own a cabin on the western edge of an island in Maine. Lofty, ancient white pines and mangy, scruffy spruces ring the cabin's exterior. Through the branches, we see an expanse of water stretching toward a bluish, bell-shaped mountain on the mainland. The cabin is close enough to the ocean that we hear seals burp when they come up for air. At high tide on a breezy day, waves gently lap the rocks just below our bedroom window. It is a place without a lot of motion or commotion, peaceful and still except for the occasional osprey's sharp cry as he flies overhead or the far-off roar of a lobster boat engine as it heads out to sea. Otherwise, the quietness of woods, sky, rock, and sea prevails, cushioning the moments with a sense of removal and repose.

The air is often bleached by shafts of sunlight, fresh and sweet, that warm the grasses around the cabin on a summer morning. When I am there, I bask in the peacefulness, inhaling the quiet, smelling the deep green of the woods, tasting the sea salt in the breeze that gently cools the skin on my face. The days are as bright as the nights are black, velvet and soft, illumined only by a thousand milky stars overhead. We often lie on the night-cooling grass in front of the cabin, counting the flecks of light blinking at us from above. Once my eyes adjust to the illuminated darkness, I am comforted and enveloped in it as I slip off to sleep.

I have visited Maine in the summer since I was young, as has my husband as we both had grandmothers who lived there in the summer. Maine is where we have always gone to retreat. When I arrive each summer, the relentless metronome beat of city life fades, and my nervous system, with all its activated synapses, begins to ratchet down. The chronic stiffness in my shoulders loosens, and I can feel my muscles opening as I stretch in the sunlight. I move more slowly, often barefoot as the grasses and pine needles are kind underfoot. When I was a child in the summer, I never wore shoes, and I retrieve a bit of that childlike feeling as I wander around shoeless.

I needed this freedom when I arrived that summer. I needed space and time to be shoeless.

On those first days that summer, I sat outside on our granite stoop in the sun, watched the clouds bowl along in the noontime sky, and listened to the wind tickle the leaves of trees deep in the woods. I felt like a chrysalis, cocooned by the quiet, tucked into myself. I didn't feel a need to do much of anything, or even try to explain to myself what I was doing or not doing. I just wanted to sit still. It felt luxurious. Occasionally I slipped into sleepiness—like a Labrador curled up, dreaming in the sun. Everything slowed.

Though my husband was not yet retired, he took a leave of absence from his job that summer so he could come to Maine with me for a few months. He, however, was not inclined to slow down. Soon after we arrived at the cabin, he set about unpacking himself and his belongings, creating little to-do piles in corners and on tables—letters to write, books to read, newspaper clippings about lectures or talks to attend, lists of plants needed for the garden, and art supplies he would get for his painting and assemblage forays.

One early June morning, from my sleepy perch on the stoop, I could see him through the window, flying around our tiny cabin. His curly, silver-white hair was in disarray. He was dressed only in boxers and his favorite ten-year-old denim work shirt. He was busy, quivering with activity like a fox terrier. I could tell he was getting ready for some major action.

"Whatcha doing over there?" he called out the window.

"Not much, " I answered through the haze of sunlight and quiet. "Feeling sleepy." Then, more definitively, "I'm resting."

"Want to take a look at my plan for the garden?"

It was as if he was wagging his tail in anticipation. Planning stuff and then talking about it excites him, and he is always confident that I will join in his enthusiasm for future activity.

"And then we can go to Lamoine to buy plants and talk to that guy about why the fruit trees are dying and what to add to the soil this year and whether coyote urine really will keep the deer out of the garden."

He paused, expecting I would match that fox terrier energy, perky and bright, and be ready to go.

"I trust you completely to choose the best plants possible for this season. You always do such a great job with the garden and I am never very good at choosing the right plants."

At this point, he stuck his head out the window and peered at me. Realizing I was not in motion, he pulled on a pair of bluejeans, gathered the necessary items for a trip to Lamoine, and sauntered out to my stoop and sat. He fixed me with that speculative look he had whenever he noticed unusual and—what he considered—questionable behavior on my part. He crossed his arms over his chest.

"You aren't going anywhere for a while, are you?"

"Nope. I want to just sit here, at least for a time."

He nodded slowly, considering. "So *this* is retirement? Doing nothing. Sitting and staring? *Resting*?? This is not like you."

This is just the kind of reaction I was worried about, I thought. *People aren't used to me not being busy, active. Engaged. Will I be able to hold out for something new in the face of friends and family pushing me to get busy? ECK!*

"That's just the point. I don't want to be like me right now. I want to find out what it's like *not* to be like me. And the first step seems to be for me to sit still and not get busy right away."

"How long is this going to go on?"

From his perspective, sitting still was something to be avoided at all costs—a sign of illness or something worse. He felt sorry for me. He looked more closely at me. I was wearing only a threadbare turquoise muumuu I had bought in a thrift shop in my '40s and a straw cowboy hat we had gotten at the last cowboy poetry night at our gym. No underwear, no shoes. I could see him taking in my frowsy, un-put-together state.

"I have no idea," I said. "But I am quite content just sitting here, for the moment. Giving myself permission not to hurry anywhere or anything."

He sighed, stood up, and threw me a doleful look. "Well ... okay. If that's what makes you happy for now, go for it."

With that, he spun around, grabbed the garden plans, recycled shopping bags, and car keys he had dropped on the grass, and headed for the driveway. "But *I* better get going."

He was sure that *somebody* had to keep moving! "There's *so* much to do," was his parting shot.

As I watched the car disappear up the dirt road without me, I had to wonder what was going on with me. Normally, invigorated upon arrival in this summer place where I could do things I couldn't do in the city, I would have by now hiked around Little Long Pond and made sure we had a breakfast picnic on top of Beech Mountain. I would have gone back to the YMCA in the nearby town for a jazzercise class and afterward to the health food store for a peach and sunflower seed muffin. Sooner or later, I would have made a plan to take the ferry out to the little island nearby so we could walk across the stone beach to the lighthouse.

But so far, I had done none of these things and hadn't felt any need to. It was enough, this time, for me to sit and watch the silty grey-green water ebb out of the cove as the tide went out and to notice how many different shades of green glimmered in the woods when the sun moved through the trees at different times of the day. It was a strangely comfortable way to be spending time just then, at the beginning of that summer.

If this was what free fall felt like, then I was grateful to be in it. For me, it was a chance to let go of conscious control or direction for a while and not rush to fill in the blanks. Liberated limbo.

Transition guru and author William Bridges calls this kind of time a "neutral zone—a gap in the continuity of existence," when the old way of being in the world no longer fits and a new direction or identity has yet to be found. It is a time for uncoupling oneself from what one knows and depends on to define oneself in the world. It takes time, patience, and a commitment to letting go of the familiar and allowing nothing to be there for a while, emptying what has been assumed about one's life in order to make room for what else might happen.

Suzanne Braun Levine, in her book *Inventing the Rest of Our Lives*, calls such a time the "Fertile Void"—a "gravity-free zone" in which "nothing grounds you but the present." This nothing time is rich with potential because it is not cluttered with old habits of being and thinking. And, apparently, if we don't rush to fill in the gap and re-identify ourselves too quickly, something perhaps unexpected and more fitted to who one is becoming will take root.

I didn't yet fully understand how essential it was to stay in this neutral zone for a time, nor did I have any idea where it would lead me. But I did sense that something unfamiliar and open-ended was happening inside me. My body felt loose, light, spacious. I was stilled but dreaming. I liked the sensation as I sat on my stoop that June.

Needless to say, initially, my inactivity seemed a lack of motivation. Floatiness was unsettling to outside observers. It wasn't merely my husband who noticed. People were used to me being active, energetic, voluble—not dozing in the sun Labrador-like. This unnerved them. They expected me to get moving.

My daughter was the most direct. She assumed that, upon retiring, I'd be unable to deal with not having anything to do and thus would nervously but efficiently figure out what was next. One day in June, she called during her lunch hour.

"Hi, Mom. How's retirement? It's been a month. Are you going crazy worrying about what to do next?"

"No. Not yet, anyway."

"So ... what *are* you doing with yourself? Have you seen the cousins? Talked to Grandma? Have you been up a mountain? Are you painting? Making plans for what you're going to do when you get home?"

"In fact, I haven't done any of those things. I'm not doing anything much, just sitting around in the sun ... thinking ..."

"What do you mean you aren't doing anything?" Her voice raised an octave. "That's not like you. What's going on? You aren't acting like yourself. Are you depressed? Or sick? Early dementia??"

This was a joke, I think.

"No. I'm not sick or depressed and, you're right, I'm not acting like myself."

What else could I say?

There were other awkward conversations with people who were in the habit of talking with me every summer about work. My serious-minded physical therapist cousin and I spoke when I saw her in late June. Each summer we'd take a beach walk together, heads down, walking into the wind, talking a mile a minute. We'd update each other on where we were professionally and what we were going to do next, and end by reflecting on how important our work lives were to us, just as they had been to our fathers who were brothers.

"So what's next? Now that you've closed your practice, are you going to teach or consult or write or what?" my cousin asked.

When I said that I didn't know, that I hadn't figured all

that out yet, my cousin turned her most concerned, wide-and-surprised, brown eyes on me for a moment and then, quickly, turned to look out to sea as if she could find an explanation out there for my hapless attitude. "How come you don't know? Haven't you had enough time to think about it and decide?"

I felt what a college senior must feel when people ask repeatedly what they will do after graduation. I didn't have answers for these questions and somehow, saying that I didn't yet know didn't satisfy anyone.

It took a while, but after almost a month of this Labrador-like lounging, I did get restless. It suddenly wasn't always comfortable for me to stay in this dreamlike, floating state. I bugged myself to get going, make a plan. In these moments, I wanted my future to take shape and to leave behind the uncertainty. *Maybe I could join that group that has people over fifty tutoring kids in reading?* I would think. *Or apply to the Georgetown program in executive coaching. I like coaching,* I thought, *and it would give me something to say when people asked me what I was doing.* Or I would fantasize about becoming a writer, not that I had any idea how to do that.

But I resisted fastening onto one of these ideas right away. This is what I had done in the past during transitions whenever I was uncertain about what to do next—decide in advance what I would do, make a plan, and make it happen sooner rather than later so there would be no gaps, no empty, undefined time. I rushed into things; I got married when I was twenty-two, barely out of college.

I went back to graduate school classes six weeks after my son was born. I got new jobs before I quit old ones. I have never liked in-between periods. I was determined to do this transition differently. I wasn't going to rush this process of change despite my restlessness. Regularly, that feisty gremlin, living somewhere deep inside my brain now, would pipe up in a chirpy voice, reminding me that I was not only retiring from my work life but from the way I used to do things. It was time to live life in a new way. This was my chance!

Soon after this, early one morning, I stood at the old-fashioned tin sink in our cabin, fiddling with the dripping faucet and thinking about the fact that, since I hadn't been to the grocery store, we only had sardines and pickles for lunch. I distracted myself by turning on the radio. It was Terry Gross on Fresh Air talking to someone about the work and wisdom of Oliver Sacks. The interview ended with a quote from one of his books:

"To be ourselves we must re-possess our life-stories. We must recollect ourselves, recollect the inner drama, the narrative. We need such a narrative, a continuous inner narrative, to maintain and clarify our identity at different stages of our lives."

Something clicked in my brain. That's what I wanted to do now, with all this retired time and future freedom. Now that I didn't belong to a work life or even to a tumultuous family life, my kids having truly fledged, I was free—free to re-possess myself, recollect what had been, and rethink what might be.

A vague sense of direction, a glimmer like light at dawn, appeared on the horizon of my sleepy brain—not quite the North Star, but a whiff of something compelling.

I had been waiting for this moment to arrive when I felt ready to do something other than sit still. It was almost August, and I was ready for more action. It was time for me to get off my stoop and to get moving, to forge ahead someway or another. I wanted to throw myself into the re-possessing of my future ... whatever that was going to be.

I'll go to the library, I decided. Libraries have always, one way or another, helped me focus.

I left the faucet dripping, left my frowsy t-shirt and shorts in a heap, threw on some going-to-town clothes, and headed out, waving to my husband in his garden on the way to the car. I even brushed my hair.

There is a library in almost every town or village in Maine, each one different from the next. On Mt. Desert, an island of 108 square miles, there are eight. The Northeast Harbor Library is light and airy—expansive with many rooms and tables, corner desks, and chairs to settle into. It is also often empty, so when I go there, I feel as if I have the place to myself. I enjoy talking with the librarians as I get to hear about how the town manager is handling the issue of replacing the sewer system and who is rebuilding on Main Street after the terrible fire. So, for this exploratory foray out from my sleepy perch at home, I chose the library in Northeast Harbor.

That afternoon, after wandering around in the upstairs stacks looking for books that might help me flesh out what re-possessing myself in retirement might look like, I meandered downstairs and ran into Brooke, the head librarian. She is small-boned and wispy-haired, and on this day was wearing a pin that said "Some books are to be tasted, others to be swallowed, and some few to be chewed and digested." We spent a few minutes musing about which books we thought should be chewed and digested and then, as usual, began to catch up on what was new for each of us.

She was surprised to hear I had retired but, unlike my friends from home, she didn't ask me what I was going to do next. Instead, she congratulated me. And then she told me about a mutual friend—a hard-nosed, taciturn, longtime lobster fisherman who the year before had sold his boat and stopped working.

"You know what Jim did when he retired?" she asked. "You won't believe it."

"What?" I imagined he ran in more marathons now that he had time on his hands.

"He's taken up bird carving. He's learning from Ed Hawkes and works every morning in the studio with Ed. He even entered his latest carving—of a hawk—in a competition in Portland."

This shocked me. My crusty, physically over-active, practical, non-artistic (or so I thought) lobster fisherman friend trying out something so thoroughly outside his wheelhouse? Taking a flier at being an artist—a woodcarver. Wow!

Jimmy's reinvention of himself was so unexpected to me. He had always been purposeful, work-oriented, and civic-minded. Over the many years that I had known him, he was very busy, involved in the community when he wasn't out fishing. He had been on the town planning board and head selectman for the town of Mt. Desert and had also served on the high school board for many years. I had never thought of him having an artistic bent. How had this transformation happened? And what had it taken for him to take such a leap, to make such a major shift?

After talking to Brooke, I drifted into the Reading Room, where there are huge, well-worn, big-footed leather couches. I dove into one of these, intrigued by what I had just heard, and I needed a moment to take stock. As I sat cushioned in this quiet room, I felt excited, inspired even, and at the same time, momentarily envious. I loved the idea of Jim going out on this entirely new, creative limb. It was so different from what he had done before. That radical difference appealed to me.

Driving home, I distractedly stared up at the bluish, darkening mountain shadowing the road, my head full of questions. *Could I do something like that? Could I do something so entirely outside* my *wheelhouse as Jim had?*

In his 2012 New Yorker article *The Disappeared*, Salmon Rushdie posed the question: "How does newness enter the world?" I loved that question and have revisited it again and again for the last many years. This was the last question I asked myself on that midsummer evening drive home. What opens you up to true newness? What allows you to break away from the familiar habits, interests, and pastimes and try out something new? How is it done? How did others do it? How would I do it?

This was a turning point. The Labrador part of me that had been snoozing finally woke up and was now interested in digging for that buried tennis ball of thinking about how we navigate our way into new futures. What did this opened-up time in my life—this 'retirement freedom'—offer? Maybe I would wear purple velvet, take up welding, write a novel, join the Peace Corps. Who knew? But I was more and more determined to be open to what I might not have imagined—to try living and learning in new ways when I got home in the fall.

I began to ask myself questions that challenged me to think differently about things I thought I already understood.

- What seems important now that wasn't before?
- What will I consider success or fulfillment to look like in the future?
- What interests me now that didn't before?

And finally:

- Who am I if I am no longer who I used to be?

I knew there were no simple answers to these questions.

For the next month, I bounced around, doing those things I had always done in Maine in the summer. I climbed mountains, visited my husband's cousins and mother, took the ferry out to the island with the lighthouse, went to the YMCA in Bar Harbor, and picnicked hither and yon. Differently than usual, I also spent more time going back to libraries, having conversations with whoever would engage with me on the subject of retirement, looking for books on this new stage of life. And then, always, back to the quiet of the cabin for more thinking, trying to answer some of the questions that kept popping up. Most of all I wondered: what did this future of mine—empty as it seemed—hold?

By late August, I still had few answers and no idea what I would do once I got back to busy Washington. Frankly, the thought of it made me very nervous. What would it be like to be back there and retired and unsure of what I would do next? To be still looking for a new narrative? But I felt ready to go back to Washington and find out.

Before we could leave, of course, we needed to close up the cabin. I am constantly impressed during these putting-away and packing-up times at how happily my husband throws himself into the process. One moment he is digging up garlic from his garden to take back to D.C., another moment he's got his head in the refrigerator, enthusiastically throwing away half-used mustards, catsups, wads of butter, and flat seltzer bottles. He scatters mothballs in drawers, crams closets with plastic-wrapped bedding, and doggedly loads and deploys mousetraps. This is a level of flurried activity that I have endeavored to match for as long as we have been married, but all too frequently I fall short. Again this year, I followed in his energetic wake, hoping some of his energy and focus might just rub off and get me ready to return to the frenetic, fast-moving pace of Washington D.C. in the fall.

At one point, my husband momentarily interrupted his tornado of cleaning and closing and looked back at me as I half-heartedly stuffed pillows into bureau drawers and threw a couple of sheets over the couch.

"I guess you aren't altogether different even though you say you aren't the same as you were before you retired. Some things just don't change, do they?"

No, I thought. I was never going to be very domestic but, beyond that, all bets were off.

Chapter Seven
Re-entry

Washington D.C. is a formidable place in early September. It would be an understatement to say it is busy. It reeks of busyness and significant, vital activity. On sharp, cracklingly sunny mornings during rush hour, buttoned-up, put-together, younger people crowd the grey sidewalks of my neighborhood, sinuous scarves wound around their necks and foreheads creased, their heads bent as they bear down on the steep subway escalator. No one smiles or chats happily—at least not first thing in the morning. In fact, no one is talking; they are too busy looking at their phones. Few look up to notice the Whitman quote engraved on the curving granite wall encircling the Dupont Circle escalator that ends: *I recall the experience sweet and sad.*

Jet black, official-looking SUVs vie for space with lesser compact cars and red taxis on the already clogged streets. They barrel through yellow lights, hell-bent on getting to the office buildings or the underground garage downtown.

There is not as much honking here in D.C. as there is in New York City. Instead, the ambient soundtrack of this city is the whine of police escort sirens in the distance, the squeak-hiss of double-sized buses as they careen into the bus stops, and the overhead whop-whop of a helicopter going to and from the White House or elsewhere. This emblematic Washington noise—thrumming, whining, airborne—leaves little chance to hear the satisfied chirping of tufty, fat sparrows burrowed back in the hedge outside my front door or the late summer cicada buzz from the tree branches above.

In my part of town at 9 AM, people are moving too fast to notice much. Not the sunlight glinting in the puddles along the curb left from last night's thunderstorm, or the flock of pigeons pecking and fighting over breadcrumbs in the tiny triangle of grass across from the subway entrance. These people, intent on whatever important work they are about to tackle, move with a determined sense of direction, heels clicking briskly on pavement, rushing to get where they are going and avoid being delayed on the way, except perhaps by that stop at Starbucks for the vanilla soy extra shot latte.

Washington in September positively vibrates with purpose and importance.

Newly returned from my free-floating summer away from the action, I was at first thrown off by the fast and furious pace of things in this city. Amidst all the hurry and directedness, I felt like a fish out of water. I was going so much slower than everyone else. And I had no specific place I had to be. How unfamiliar it felt. This was not how I knew how to live in D.C. in September. Normally I'd be revving up, getting ready to jump into the fray and bolt back to work. But this September was different than all my other D.C. Septembers. I was not returning to a workplace or a work identity—not speeding up.

The first mornings back from Maine, wanting to keep up the habit of being outdoors first thing in the morning, I would go for a walk. Donning the misshapen, old sunhat and ratty jogging shoes I had worn all summer, I would venture out the front door of our apartment building, check in with the sparrows happily feeding in the hedge, and then step onto the Connecticut Avenue sidewalk. But I realized quickly on these walks that maintaining a leisurely pace in the face of the accelerating energy of the rush-hour crowd was daunting.

One morning I was passed first by a striding woman in a tight black skirt and Adidas sneakers. She blew by me with an annoyed "excuse me." Behind her, coming on even faster, was a tall, skinny young man in a dark suit and yellow tie, head down, briefcase in hand, barreling along as if his life depended on it. As I stepped out of their way, I almost fell over the green fire hydrant hidden in the grass along the sidewalk. I was clearly off-balance in the face of this hurrying crowd. It was a little like finding oneself standing still in the middle of a road where a major race is being run. The passing runners pant with purpose and occasionally sideswipe the disoriented person dumb enough to stand still in the middle of a race. *Why wasn't I joining the race?* I wondered. It was so tempting, so seductively attractive, almost irresistible not to join them, to speed up and walk as if I had somewhere to go.

Once again I had to argue with the stern, guilt-inducing voice who urged me to reset myself after my sleepy summer, to speed up, join the throng, and hurry somewhere, anywhere! *No, no! NO!!* I would say to myself in these weak moments. *I am just out for a healthy morning walk. I don't need to hurry. I don't need to keep up with all these people bound for the office. I don't even have an office to go to.*

So I would do my best to resist the urge to hurry up and instead amble down the hill slowly, trying to hold onto the sense of living moment to moment and paying closer attention to what else there was to notice on this busy street—smelling the air, blinking in the sharp sunlight, and listening for sounds beyond the thrum of plane, car, bus, helicopter. Going slower meant I could eavesdrop whenever I came upon a conversation as I navigated the sidewalk. Mostly what I heard were one-sided phone conversations:

"Can you believe she had the nerve to dump that on me? It was her assignment; she is the Metro person, after all."

"We'll have to conference you in tomorrow but the work product needs to be on my desk close of business today."

"I hate Mondays ... don't you?"

Could I really live in this city and not have a career? I wondered often in those early fall days. And could I stave off the overwhelming anxiety aroused by the hurly-burly going on around me? Could I resist my tendency to get busy when I became anxious and just make a plan in order to be able to say I had a plan?

That first month back, I flailed. Many of my old compensatory behaviors kicked in when, after too much contact with all the hustle and bustle, I'd feel the familiar frantic fluttering in my gut, a sure signal that I needed to do SOMETHING, anything, just get moving.

In the past, making to-do lists had always calmed me down. I discovered that I made my best lists when I was hunkered down in nearby coffee shops and eateries. One day, as I was sitting in the window bench seat at Dolcezza, Gelato and Coffee shop on Connecticut Avenue staring out at the passing rush-hour throng, I decided that instead of a 'to-do' list, I needed to make a 'to-be' list. My list that day was titled, "Self Description 2012" and included the following possibilities: What I might be in the future: A Thought leader? Transition consultant? Educator? Promoter? Culture broker? I didn't even know what a *culture broker* was, but it sounded like something an older person might become. Comforted for the time being, the fluttering in my gut slowed to a dull, repetitive clench.

On another day, in a dark corner at Teaism on R Street, I made another list. This one was titled "Goals – 2012" and identified only verbs: "to re-set, to re-cast, to re-define, to free up, to upend." What I planned to upend or re-define or free up wasn't clear at that point, but at least I had some action items down on paper. I definitely felt better. That stiff-necked, wiry Puritan sitting on my shoulder urged me on, telling me with ever-accelerating emphasis to hurry up and get busy doing something worthwhile.

This 'worthwhile' narrative was a familiar message from my past. Of paramount importance, when I was growing up was to be PRODUCTIVE—to be an active and fully-engaged citizen, and to spend your days making a contribution to your community and the world. Navel-gazing and introspective, inactive time were taboo; you were missing out on everything if you were sitting still, not engaged with life outside your home.

But it was just these messages and dictates from my past that I was questioning now, along with the general workaholic culture of Washington D.C. Was I okay if I didn't immediately fill my days with worthwhile, good-citizen activity? And what if whatever I ended up doing now didn't qualify as being purposeful or making a contribution to the world? Could I become more creative about how I spent my time? Could I find a new way to be purposeful without being driven?

Questions abounded. Answers were still elusive.

In response, that other voice, the energetic gremlin voice, staunch champion of my retirement, again chirped in my other ear. "You've retired, remember? You're taking some time to find your way to doing something new with your life!" Then, even louder, "Don't panic and rush into doing something just because you won't wait to figure out what else there is to do that you haven't thought of yet."

Oh yeah. I needed the reminder. *I'm a work in progress … reinventing myself. Nobody ever said it would be easy or fast.* I needed to ignore the clench in my stomach and stay the course. And, truth be told, I liked being told not to do anything too fast. I wasn't ready to throw myself into anything yet. I needed time to figure out what might be possible, but I didn't know yet what that was going to be.

I decided it would be helpful to talk to some other retired people and find out how they had done this thing called retirement while still living in Washington D.C. I wanted to know what others did after they finished doing what they used to do—and how they felt about it.

I called my friend Elisabeth, who had retired two years

earlier. She and her husband were economists and had had a business advising companies about pricing pharmaceuticals. I figured that was a pretty big and self-defining job, and I remembered how absorbed in her work she had been. How had she decided what she would do after?

"The truth is," she said, "I was so pissed at the way the company that bought us out treated me after the sale that I was glad to quit. After I quit I plunged headfirst ... into painting, that is. And now all I do is paint."

Now that I thought about it, the last time I had seen her she had multiple vermillion paint chips in her bangs.

"But how did you figure out that painting was what you wanted to do?" I hoped she had some sort of formula for how she decided.

"I didn't think much about it, actually, on purpose. I didn't try to figure it out. That was what I did all the time as an economist—figure things out, analyze data, and make decisions based on facts. I wanted to use a different part of my brain. I wanted to follow my intuition, not the data. Be a creative instead of a numbers wonk."

She paused and then added brightly, "Now I just don't think the way I used to. I take art courses and then I go into the backroom and stay there all day trying to get better at painting. I'm still driven. I'm working just as hard as I did in my job." She laughed. "My husband wishes it wasn't so much like a new full-time job. He wants me to play more golf!"

I was inspired by the way she had made this leap, how completely she had plunged into her new endeavor, and what a total and unambivalent departure this was from what she had done before.

My friend Joan had a different approach to retirement.

I met her at Dolcezza early one morning after a leisurely saunter down Connecticut Avenue. Joan had been a lawyer and then a judge in D.C. Superior Court and had retired in the last year at 61. She has thick, curling, silver-gray hair that spills over her shoulders and always wears splashy, dangling earrings that swing as she talks.

"I got great advice from someone before I retired," she said. "A friend of my father's—a wise man—told me to wait a year before I decided what I would do next. So that's what I've done." She smiled, her earrings jingling happily. "People keep asking me what I do with my time. I tell them I go for long walks. 'How long?' they ask. 'Several hours,' I say, and then they don't ask me anything else."

"So you aren't worried about filling up your time with meaningful activity? You don't care if you aren't useful and busy at the moment?"

"Not in the least. I paid my dues. Now I get to be in the world in a different way. Having all this time and the freedom to choose what I'll do minute-to-minute means I'm simply in the present in a way I haven't been in the past."

She looked dreamily out the window as people streamed along the sidewalk on their way to the subway.

"My mind is no longer cluttered with all the shoulds and should-nots and long to-do lists about work. Right now, I'm in a trance. I read and walk. And travel. I feel more alive to stuff I haven't paid attention to in years—birdsong, the colors of winter, architecture of old neighborhoods in D.C. like LeDroit Park, talking with people about what's important to them beyond work and the weather."

She finished with another swing of those iridescent earrings and a beatific grin.

"I am doing just fine."

She sure seemed fine to me. Calm, content, clear—able to go slow or be still even amidst the busyness of this town. Staying true to her own internal, slowed-down rhythms. Buddha-like. A great role model for nervous-Nellie-me.

These women had radically changed their way of being in the world and now seemed absorbed in their new experiences of themselves and their present lives. Of course, it helped that they didn't have to worry about money, that they could take this leap unencumbered by financial pressures.

But how did they do this? How did they let the newness in?

They had done it, I had to admit, by truly letting go of what had been. Stepping off the treadmill of the familiar and approaching their future lives with the only expectation being that everything could be different, opening themselves to the unexpected with no preconditions.

This felt very Zen-like to me with some basic precepts: open-mindedness, comfort with uncertainty, freedom from long-held opinions about what one should be doing, readiness to try unfamiliar ways of being in the world and to try out things you've never done before, and finally, a tolerance for not knowing where you are headed or where you might end up. Truly dwelling, for the time being, in possibility.

I wanted to adopt a page out of *this* playbook for the coming months.

I needed to calm down and remember that change is a

verb, an ongoing process ... it doesn't necessarily happen as fast as we would like. I knew this already but needed help applying it to myself in the midst of this transition. Talking to Joan and Elizabeth helped. And, ironically, so did slowing down, or sitting still and being quiet. This gave me a chance to work at just being present to whatever was around me then; to take more time to notice sounds, colors, textures, tastes, and other things you don't notice when you are in a hurry, while I waited to find out what I might do with my freedom.

This began to make a difference. I looked more and saw more. I read more and thought more. I relaxed, and because of this loosening-up on myself, I began to unfurl.

Chapter Eight
Unfurling

To unfurl:
To unfold, expand, open out, open up, spread out.
To make or become spread out from a rolled or folded state,
especially in order to be open to the wind.

When I was a kid in the summer, I loved sailing with my family. Back then, my family owned a 21-foot, wooden, one design sailboat, and most summer days when my father could be with us in Maine, we went on sailing picnics to near beaches or faraway islands.

Putting up the sails was a major undertaking, especially when the wind was up. The dirty canvas sail bags housed the stiff, bunched-up mainsail and jib. After lugging them out of the rocking dingy and onto the slatted bottom of the sailboat, we'd lean in and yank them out, clutching them to our chests in bear-hug fashion, wrapping our arms around their bulk to prevent the wind from whipping them around and out of the boat before we had clipped them to the halyards. The challenge was to keep them furled (curled and folding into themselves) and still (untouched as yet by the nattering windiness) until they were fully attached and we could raise them—first the mainsail and then the jib—and watch as they slowly or suddenly—depending on the wind's velocity that day—filled up with the breeze, caught the wind, and began to pull us out of the harbor. Then we could sit back and look up at those previously furled sails, now becoming more fully unfurled—ballooned out, expansive, open to the wind and sun.

I had returned to Washington that September furled, having spent the summer curling into myself as a way to retreat from my former life and my old habits of being. Now that I was back in D.C. and had survived the initial overwhelm of reentry to this frenetically busy city, I finally began to unfurl. I was free in a way I hadn't been since I was young. I was lucky enough not to have financial pressure to earn money at this point, so I didn't have to find another job. Thankfully I was also healthy, not yet challenged by the inevitable physical limitations that eventually come with aging.

Different and sometimes unsettling as this kind of freedom—freed-up time—felt, I knew what a bonanza it was—how infrequently one gets to have such open-ended, unstructured time and space, unburdened from responsibilities, afflictions, and obligations. I began to not worry that my days weren't filled with activity or that I wasn't revving up to do some kind of major project. I stopped trying to figure out what I would say to people when they asked me what I was doing now that I was retired and even stopped asking myself the same question.

I didn't plan. I let myself be ...

I found I liked thinking of this time in my life as an unfurling—an opportunity to literally loosen up and open out, to slowly fill up with whatever was to happen next now that I had let go of so much. In the meantime, I would be still—fending off the nervous need to get busy—until I could get my bearings and set a course for myself in this new time.

I spent more and more time in the backroom of our apartment, away from the harried, hurrying subway-bound crowds and the noise of the city. Often I seemed idle, sitting still in the honey-colored, red-cushioned wicker chair I had brought to our apartment from the screened-in porch of our old house. Tucking into that chair afforded me a sense of enclosure, comfort, and being where I needed to be while I thought my unfurling thoughts. Sometimes it was downright strange to spend so much time with myself, alone and still, but more often I felt as if I was marinating in this new experience of time.

I continued to search out and read everything positive I could find about this time of life. I shunned the gloom and doom narratives about the myriad problems and challenges associated with aging and the cautionary tales about the emptiness of retirement. The books I read were upbeat and encouraging—insisting we revise our thinking about what is possible and even—in many ways—better about this stage of life.

Marc Freedman, founder of Encore.org and author of *The Big Shift*, urged those of us of a certain age and post-retirement to see this phase of life as one full of opportunity and creativity. We must, he suggests, "inhabit an emerging life course, muster the imagination and will to forge a new map of life fitted to the new length of life, and to the particular circumstances and opportunities of the twenty-first century."

In her book *Composing a Furthur Life*, Catherine Bateson, cultural historian, author, and daughter of Margaret Mead, called this time of life—after someone has given up a lifelong career and the associated responsibilities, obligations, and preoccupations—"a second and different kind of adulthood that precedes old age." As a result of "unprecedented levels of health, energy, time and resources," she said, those of us now over 60 have the opportunity to be full participants in an entirely new developmental life stage she called the *age of active wisdom*.

I was fully aware, as I read this, that not everyone over 60 had what she called "unprecedented levels of health, energy, time, and resources." Many people I knew didn't have the financial security to retire anytime soon. More and more of my contemporaries were having hip replacements. There were many discussions about loss— of eyesight, memory, physical strength, general health ... and, even more seriously, about the loss of friends. A dear friend had died of prostate cancer. My younger cousin had open-heart surgery to fix a prolapsed valve and still had trouble catching her breath. Another friend was battling heart disease and could hardly walk up the stairs.

I too was old for sure, but I didn't feel old in the way I thought I would. I had to admit I was heavier and slower now that I was older. When I woke up some mornings, I was stiff and creaky. I had wrinkles galore and bags under my eyes, and I wasn't as tall as I used to be, but that hadn't translated into my feeling like a doddering, over-the-hill old person. And, despite the fact I had trouble retrieving the name of a person I had known for twenty years when I saw her at the market in my neighborhood, my mind still seemed intact, as far as I could tell.

Being this age was better than I had anticipated. If I was lucky enough to be healthy and free—for the time being, anyway—I couldn't wait to find out how to be "actively wise" as well. I wanted to cultivate the possibilities of being this age and retired rather than just resign myself to being "put out to pasture"—a conventional societal message to seniors.

These books gave me new perspectives on what I was doing—being still, thinking, and reading in my chair—and on what I might look forward to in the future. I was mentally unfurling into a new experience of myself.

In contrast, when we returned to Washington after the summer in Maine, my husband had busily gone back to work. On most days, I would catch glimpses of his wild white head of hair—now long from a summer away from the barber—as he orbited around in his hurried doingness, in and out of the apartment, traveling to meetings or his office, or at home, on the phone or the computer. Commenting in passing about various projects and obligations, huffing and puffing at the stress of keeping all the balls in the air that he had set in motion. And, at the end of many days, coming to rest in the opposite wicker chair in my study, tired and complaining about how behind the eight ball he felt and how much he had to do.

"What are *you* doing with yourself all day?" he asked one blustery October evening. "You don't seem to be accomplishing anything." My husband has the same stiff-back, black-hatted Puritan sitting on his shoulder as I do—one who rails about being productive and useful in the world and reminds us frequently that 'idle hands are the work of the Devil.'

"Well ..." I said, feeling a little embarrassed and called out, as if I was breaking some sort of unwritten rule that says, if you live in Washington D.C., sooner or later you HAVE to get busy so you look like you are accomplishing something meaningful—even if you aren't. "I'm not quite sure how to answer that." I was groping, trying to explain as much to myself as to him what wasn't yet clear. "I've never ever spent so much time being quiet, still and by myself ..." I paused, surprised by that thought, "and it's so unfamiliar that I don't recognize myself in it. But it's *good* stillness—a kind of *exploratory quiet*. I think something is happening but I just don't know what it is yet."

He leaned toward me and ran his fingers through his rumpled hair. "But what are you DOING?" he said with mock bewilderment. "I thought when you got back to D.C. you would get busier," he went on, sounding now legitimately surprised. "Are you happy going so slow? Spending so much time alone? Doing so little?" He gaped at me for a moment as if he had met an alien in the corner drugstore. He was used to a BUSY me—crazily multitasking, having too many things to do rather than too little.

"Oh, I am busy, believe me," I replied, rearranging myself in my chair and sitting up straighter. Now I began to feel scrappy and a little heated. "I am busy cultivating a new way to be me. I just haven't figured it all out yet, haven't pulled it and my new self together." I went on, nodding my head, hoping I sounded and looked very sure about what I wasn't at all sure about.

"So," I said, knowing that if I lapsed into psycho-babble it would drive him crazy and put an end to this conversation, "Rest assured, something is happening over here. You may not recognize it but I'm in the process of ..." I sputtered, "of *de-familiarizing* myself with what went before and *re-constellating* my reality while I 're-possess' myself."

He scowled at me, shrugged, launched himself up out of the chair, and suggested we have a cocktail. I couldn't have agreed more.

What I didn't say that evening was that I was beginning to get a sense of what I wanted to do next, of how I might re-engage in the world in a way that had new meaning for me. I was thoroughly taken with the notion— put forth in most of the books I had been reading—that this time of life offered great opportunities for reinvention, renewal, and actual "re-wirement" as suggested in Miners and Sedlar's *Don't Retire, Rewire!* Mark Walton, in his book *Boundless Potential; Transform your Brain, Unleash Your Talents, Reinvent Your Work in Midlife,* suggests that, in midlife and beyond, success takes on a different meaning for people willing to venture beyond what is familiar and well-known to them. The men and women he describes in the book have "set out to reinvent their earlier success by creating a new kind of work they truly love." In doing so, they find their way to what he calls "reinventive work— self-created endeavors that unlock our unique lifetime potential, provide the highest levels of happiness, and have a meaningful impact in the world." Both Walton and Sarah Lawrence-Lightfoot, who wrote *The Third Chapter: Passions, Risk and Adventure in the 25 Years*

After 50, tell compelling stories about the potential for transformations and 'creative and purposeful learning' that can happen as a result of people springing free in the second half of their lives.

I loved reading these stories. But it was no longer enough just to read about these folks. It had been so helpful to talk to Joan and Elisabeth. I was ready to get out again and talk to more people about all of this. I wanted to see for myself how people who had retired "forged new life maps," as Marc Freedman suggested, or became "full participants in an entirely new life stage" and "actively wise"—the unanticipated possibilities described by Catherine Bateson for new endeavors at this stage of life.

So I set about it. Who else did I know who had retired and what did they have to tell me?

I called this endeavor my Retirement Project (probably to give it some legitimacy in my own mind and some cover from those who continued to wonder whether I would ever reactivate, get busy, and do something). I explained to friends and colleagues that, while I had no idea what I would do with the information I was collecting, I was simply intrigued with the subject of retirement and reinvention. I used this as an explanation for why I wanted to 'formally interview' them, if they were willing, to hear their perspectives and stories about retirement.

I re-grouped. And got busier. And out of my chair.

Chapter Nine
Retirement Stories
Take-offs and Landings

John Wimberly was my first quarry. John has a crop of silvery hair, a bushy mustache, and red cheeks. He smiles with his eyes. He could be a stand-in for Santa.

He had retired the previous Christmas Eve after forty years as a Presbyterian minister and had not, it seemed, let the grass grow underneath him as he careened full-bore into this new opened-up stage of his life. These days, when he was not in Mexico being a potter, he was working as a consultant to churches around the country helping them do strategic planning and financial management. He had also just started a short-term stint as the editor of a magazine—something he says he had no idea how to do.

John and I were sitting at a pockmarked wooden table in his kitchen. As we began to talk, a wiry, dun-colored blind cat that he and his wife had brought home from Mexico climbed up on the table. She lay between us, tail switching, turning her head toward John and then quickly toward me, as if listening for our words.

"I like being this old!" he said, clearly delighted with the notion. He was 70 at the time. "I love being the oldest person in the conversation. I feel like I know stuff. And I get a kick out of sharing what I know when people ask my advice. And saying things no one else will—like talking about worse case scenarios or giving advice to people they don't want to hear. They can take it or leave it. The best part is that I don't have to be responsible anymore for the outcomes. I'm free!"

He stroked the Mexican cat and got more serious.

"Even though I treasure those forty years of ministry, I don't miss anything about being a pastor now. It turns out the car was out of gas even before I recognized it so I am glad I finally got out and walked away."

He paused, thinking back on this.

"I had no idea how much stress I was carrying until I let go of the job. Somehow or other, I thought I was solely responsible for making the world a different place and for everyone's happiness. Can you imagine what a boon it is to let go of that responsibility? Now I hardly recognize myself. I'm a much more relaxed, spontaneous, free-wheeling person than I ever thought I could be ... and I can't get enough of new experiences."

"Do you mean a person has to let go of all responsibility or stress in order to get relaxed and free?"

"No. It's just that I don't have to worry so much about making things succeed or go well. Now I'm free to fail in ways I've never been!"

Free to fail? What a concept, I thought.

I had gotten to know John when we'd worked

together—he as treasurer and me as chair—on the board of a local non-profit that had a bucket-load of problems. In the end, he and I had gotten into a major disagreement with the executive director, who had resigned in a fury, blaming us for mismanagement. Those were tense times, and we'd both felt helpless to prevent the ensuing disarray in the organization. I had felt like I had failed then, and wondered if maybe John did as well.

As if he were reading my mind, he said, "Being retired gives me the time and distance to reflect on what I did and didn't do well. And it is the mistakes and failures that taught me much more than the successes."

I thought about Samuel Becket's words: "Ever tried. Ever failed. No matter. Try Again. Fail again. Fail better." I hadn't come upon this quote until after I had retired. I wish I had had the benefit of this kind of wisdom in my younger life. Failing didn't seem like an option when I was a young teacher in front of a classroom of twenty-five thirteen-year-olds. I feared they would skin me alive, laugh me out of the classroom, and, even worse, realize I didn't know what I was doing ... yet. It was my first year teaching a seventh-grade English class. We were discussing some arcane aspect of the play we had been reading, and they were bored with the discussion and getting rowdy. I turned my back to write something on the board. Someone turned off the lights and, as they say, all hell broke loose. I heard high-pitched hooting and hilarity as the kids raced out the door. So much for control of the classroom. At the time I was too embarrassed to think much about it—much less learn from it.

Later on, as a new therapist, I still didn't get how much I could learn from missteps or mistakes. I was too afraid of making the wrong choices, of fumbling in situations. I tried too hard to get up to speed fast without making blunders or falling short. I didn't want to be a beginner. I wanted to know what to do and wanted to do it well the first time I tried. As a result, in those early days with supervisors, I had trouble taking advantage of feedback. I reacted defensively and felt discouraged instead of being open to learning from my mistakes. Of course, slowly but surely, I realized how wrong-headed this notion was, but it was a painful learning curve with a lot of embarrassment and stumbles along the way.

The good news, John was saying, was that once we get to this advanced stage of life, we understand that mistakes and failures are the inevitable, excruciating ways we learn what we most need to learn, what we would never learn from what goes well. Mistakes are mirrors where we get an opportunity to see ourselves more clearly than usual.

The debacle at the non-profit had been wrenching. I was inexperienced at managing people and not used to being in charge. I also knew little then about financial management and thus felt overwhelmed by the financial challenges this organization faced. In the end, for many reasons, it became clear that I needed to resign and let the rest of the board step up and make decisions that they were unwilling to make as long as I was in charge.

"When we were on that board together, we thought we understood what was happening and could prevent disaster," John said. "We couldn't. We didn't. We failed." He smiled. "We learned a lot."

I had to agree. It felt good to have John just say it— plain and clear.

That failure had both seared and seasoned me. I had to

face my limitations squarely. The surprise was that blowing it had, in a strange way, been liberating. I couldn't hide the fact that I had failed. I had to accept it, accept that everyone knew about my failure, and find a way to move on and learn from it.

Finally, John reflected on what the freedom he felt offered him. "These days I'm only in charge of inventing my new reality. I'm doing things I've never done—like spending three months a year in Mexico making pots or learning how to edit and publish a magazine, or even figuring out how to live with my wife all over again now that we're both retired. I'm finding out what now is important to do or be."

He paused, thoughtful again, and then said, "I don't deny that the background music of this time of life is how much closer we all are to our own deaths. People we know are sick and dying. There's a lot of sadness. But for me right now there is also a lot of joy, a lot more living to be done. Whoever thought this time of life would be so full of surprises that I enjoy? It's so unexpected. I love the adventure."

There was much food for thought in what John had had to say. I wondered if a female retired minister would have a different take on this thing called retirement. So, I sought out my friend Susan, who had retired as rector of her church two years before.

I had known Susan for over thirty years since meeting her as the associate rector of a church my husband and I attended for a few years when our kids were young. Susan was my first experience with a female priest. The Episcopal church only agreed to ordain women in 1976, and I hadn't been back to any church since leaving home and going to college in 1968. I looked forward to getting to know a woman filling a role denied to her in the past and to see how she navigated this in a community unused to women being in a leadership position.

Susan had come from a traditional background and had envisioned her major role in life as a wife and mother. When she was younger, she had had no ambition or vision for herself as a professional woman. But that changed after a miscarriage and a great deal of soul searching. Her interest in Christianity intensified at that point. Eventually, she decided to enter a seminary with the goal of becoming a priest.

I include this background because, as I set out to talk to different people about retirement, I wondered whether women who had had to break out of traditional female roles to take on a profession would have a harder time giving up their professional identity as they anticipated retirement.

Susan is a soft-spoken but determined rebel. When I was going to her church in the 1990s, I loved watching the stealthy but steady way she would question some pontificating man or certain woman in the congregation. She'd smile sweetly, cock her head slightly, lean in toward the person, and calmly present an alternative idea. Or she'd question what was being said—though in the nicest of ways. Reasonable, rational, not giving up. Truth be told, I also liked that she would often wear high heels that peeked out of the bottom of her pastoral robes and that she tried to upend the Episcopal church rules about whether she could become rector after her boss left. She didn't succeed in overturning the status quo on that one, but she went on to become a rector of an even bigger church in Maryland soon after.

Susan plunged in with questions and answers.

"Want to know what I thought about and asked myself when I got ready to retire?" she asked. "I thought about how hard I had worked at becoming a good minister. The job wasn't easy, but I kept striving to get better at it for all the years I worked." She shook her head, remembering. "What, I wondered, happens to the parts of yourself you have worked so hard to develop over time in order to be good at your chosen profession? Do you have to give up those parts of yourself in order to really retire when they've been so hard-won?"

She tapped the table beside her and looked me hard in the eye. "Of course not!"

It was near dusk, and we were in a tiny study in her house, sipping wine and watching the sunlight and shadows bounce off the huge magnolia leaves in her backyard. When she is getting ready for a good conversation, Susan tucks her feet under her and leans in, intent on what is being said. She did that now as she folded herself into the corner of the couch. She is small, fit, and has the exact same short, blondish, close-cropped hairdo she had thirty years ago.

"Nobody takes that identity away from you," she said. "Yes, I retired as a full-time rector but I kept my hand in church-related stuff by preaching an occasional sermon or teaching a class in the Christian Education program at my old church or organizing a book group where we read the latest books by theologians. I still like thinking and reading and talking about theological issues."

After a moment she added, "And what I seem to care

about right now is interpreting for people what I think God is all about."

This surprised me. When I visited with Susan these days, we talked about politics, children and grandchildren, travel, and books. We never talked about God, church, or faith.

"How are you doing that?" I wondered aloud. "In what context?"

"When I retired," she said, "I was determined to try and write a little article about church for people who are alienated, who feel that going to church is irrelevant in their lives, meaningless. And to my astonishment, it has turned into a book. I was totally unprepared for this as I sure didn't think of myself as a writer, but I have loved doing it. I hope it will encourage folks to reconsider going to church."

I had always known Susan to be a great conversationalist, an extrovert who loved talking. So it made total sense when she went on to say, "I think of my writing as a conversation. And I have discovered that writing gives you a way to become part of a conversation you think is important."

I was impressed. I had a lot of respect for all Susan did as a minister. But among the many roles she had played in the past, writing a book was not in the mix. Now in retirement, she had taken what she cared about into a new forum. She elaborated and enlarged the conversation and in doing so was reaching many more people than she had as a minister.

"Now I want to write another book—about assisted suicide. My father had Alzheimer's and lived way too long. He wouldn't have wanted to live on the way he did—being so out of it."

Her face clouded over. She was serious, focused.

"People don't talk about death and what they might want if they got terribly sick until it's too late. I want to give people an opportunity to think about it. And some guidance."

Susan seemed very much at peace with herself and her present life and excited about how her wisdom and experience could be useful to others still. "I've been through a lot," she went on. "Two divorces, a failed pregnancy, money worries, parenting and job stress and responsibilities, illness and death of friends and family, a new marriage. I've proved to myself that I can not only manage a lot of life but also offer comfort and guidance that matters in the dark times. I'm proud of much of what I've done and no longer look for approval from the world." Settling herself more deeply into the couch, she said quietly, "I guess you'd call that grace."

After a minute or two, she finished: "When you get to be this old, you don't have a ten-year plan. The time horizon comes into focus; it's real, and it's inevitable. But oddly, that has totally freed me up. It has made me more willing to take risks, to take on new experiences maybe before it's too late. I feel curious and open ... and free— what a gift!"

In his book, *The Third Age,* William Sadler suggests that with the benefits of increased longevity, enhanced mobility, and financial security, this time of life can offer us the possibility of both a take-off and a landing. I came away from these conversations thinking that Susan and John were doing both. They seemed to be landing in the sense that they were at home and at peace with who they had been and who they were becoming. Their self-acceptance didn't depend on external approval or achievement.

Their take-offs, on the other hand, included new ventures into unforeseen arenas, as well as full engagement with whatever interested and compelled them in the present. Poster children for what *active wisdom* at this stage of life could mean, they were intent on passing along what they knew if people were interested in listening. They appeared to be enjoying a special kind of freedom borne of having paid their dues over many years and feeling entitled to follow their passions and unimagined pursuits, fully open to both the opportunities and challenges of life after retirement.

I loved these conversations and had many more over the next months with friends, colleagues, and strangers. A retired World Bank lawyer delighted in telling me about his early love of opera. His first LP was a recording of Carmen. Now that he was retired, he was leading tours of the costume studio of the Washington Opera and selling cokes at the consignment stand at the Kennedy Center during opera season. The husband of a good friend, who had a long and stressful career as a doctor and administrator at Kaiser, was now teaching meditation and learning to play the piano. My old supervisor at the Washington School of Psychiatry left his practice and was painting full time and showing his work in a gallery.

Many of the people I spoke to didn't like the term *retired*. "I may no longer work in the financial world but I'm sure not done!" declared a neighbor who had had a career in finance and investment. "I'm at the top of my game and have a lot to offer," she said. "Describing yourself as retired sounds like you have no energy left to do things in the world. I have just signed onto The Visitor's board at my alma mater and have joined a community advisory committee for the town of Chatham, Massachusetts."

A seventy-two-year-old retired Labor Department employee I spoke to had taken up musical theater.

"Last month," she told me gleefully, "I got a part in Guys and Dolls at a local theater. I'm one of the Dolls! Whoever thought I could go from being a drone-like civil servant to singing in a musical at my age."

I came away from these talks impressed by so many people's determination to cut loose, use their imaginations, and do things they had never done before. They often didn't know where they were headed but got aboard the train anyway and just went with it. These folks seemed like true examples of *re-wirement* in retirement.

If this was what retirement was all about, I thought, I'm all in. And I was closer than I realized to discovering my own way of 'rewiring,' and what would end up being my 'reinventive work.'

In late November of that year, I was invited to a lunchtime talk by a woman who had written a memoir about her father. I didn't usually go to author talks, even though I loved reading about writers and the writing life. So, truth be told, I only went to this one because I wanted to visit with my friend.

Before she began her talk, the long-haired, aquiline-faced author peered shyly out at the audience from behind the podium, taking her wire-rimmed glasses off her nose as she did. Her manner was oddly appealing and invited interest. She seemed at once both reserved and yet ready to engage as she stood, quietly composed, waiting for us to join her in this story.

Sara Mansfield Taber began to talk about her life as the daughter of a spy. Until she was 15, her father had told her he was a diplomat. She spoke quietly but forcefully, her story gaining momentum as the underlying reality became clearer. She read from her book, *Born Under an Assumed Name: The Memoir of a Cold War Spy's Daughter*, full of passages with luminous images and stunning metaphors:

"The sea breeze sipped at our sun-burned skins."

"One day the corset of tentativeness I had felt for months slid off me like a silky slip."

"A father's future watery-wavering-slipping away sadness."

But what affected me the most was how honest she was about herself—her vulnerabilities, her confusions, her mishaps and stumbles, as well as her insights and the way her storytelling and use of language transformed all of this into beautifully wrought art.

At the end of her talk, she mentioned that she had become a writing coach and was taking on individual clients—hoping to encourage others to get on with writing.

It felt, in that moment, as if I was being beckoned by a benevolent snake charmer, hypnotized into thinking that I could join her in this kind of new adventure. In the past, while I was a therapist, I had written several articles about my work for clinical journals, but I had never felt I could justify calling myself a writer. That was something reserved for creative people, people who wrote books. But here was a chance for me to venture into forbidden, off-the-reservation territory, to go out on a limb and try to do something I hadn't planned on or had experience with. I wanted to try this out. I wanted to take up writing seriously. Perhaps I would eventually write about all the people I had interviewed or all I had learned about the possibilities of new endeavors later in life; perhaps I would write a mystery and become the next Agatha Christie. I didn't know what might come of this, and, to my surprise, that didn't seem to matter.

So I decided, in this new life of mine, for however long I had until I was too old to think and reflect, I would "get on" with writing with the help of this serious, eloquent, aquiline-faced author as my coach and inspiration. In January of the next year, I signed up to become her writing student and mentee.

Chapter Ten
Re-Possessing Myself Through Writing

"Don't be afraid to discover what you are saying in the act of saying it." – Alice Steinbach

"A writer is not so much someone who has something to say as he is someone who has found a process that will bring out new things he would not have thought of had he not started to say *(write)* them." – William Stafford

I was excited about this new focus. I was curious to see what would happen if I spent my days taking writing seriously. What could I discover if I buckled down and gave myself up to this process? Was this going to be my way of reinventing myself?

I could see that writing—as a creative discipline and practice—could offer me a way of locating myself now that I was 63 and retired. I was different now, new to myself, and in many ways, still uncertain about how I might react or think about things in my new life. I was no longer looking at my life through the lens of professional demands, active parenting or caretaking, and had jettisoned, for the time being, my tendency to be determinedly involved and in motion in the outside world.

I wanted to rethink long-held perceptions, to go deeper than I was used to, to get beneath timeworn ways of thinking, to question myself and arrive at new conclusions based on all the change I felt in myself and in my life. And I hoped writing could provide me with a structure and an opportunity to do this.

In order to do this, I thought, I had to develop a writing practice. I needed to learn to be newly curious, to follow my thoughts and reflections wherever they would lead me, even to places I might not want to go. I needed to listen more closely for unexpected ideas or unimagined narratives that might emerge from inside myself if I could sit still and be patient.

Charles Johnston, a psychiatrist and author, said in his book, *The Creative Imperative*, "We need to take seriously what we cannot see. Creativity is a process with its own logic. We must create space for the process and have faith in it."

Space and faith ... that's what I needed. I needed the kind of space that would invite imagination. And I needed faith that something would come out of this. I needed to feel confident that despite a lack of direction, I would make discoveries along the way.

I decided to begin my writing practice by literally clearing space. I had spent time these past months in my comfortable but crowded study, curled up in the wicker armchair, books and papers piled on the floor next to me and all over every available surface in the room. Strewn about were random memorabilia—my son's first-grade ceramic tiger, a sandstone statue of a sphinx I had gotten in an antique store in Buffalo, countless framed photos of parents, children, siblings, and anyone else who mattered in my life, a watercolor I had done in Maine, and a collection of tiny, beaded leather bowls arranged and rearranged whenever I needed distraction. I loved this room with all its idiosyncratic objects and distractions. But it was time for it and me to be different. It was time for me to use this space in a new way.

So I started clearing. It helped that I had switched my morning routine from drinking sweet black tea to drinking very dark, very strong, unsweetened coffee—more akin to rocket fuel than a gentle wake-up booster. This cleared my mind and galvanized me. I committed to arriving in my study every morning I could by 9 AM, my favorite 'Seize the Day' coffee mug in hand, ready to do what it took to clear this space of mine for whatever my new writing practice needed in order to go forward.

On Day One of clearing my study, I gulped my coffee and swung into action. One by one, I stowed away the books I had read over the past year and left piled on the floor. I perched atop an unsteady stool to find space for them on the top shelf of the bookcase. The process took a while; there were many books, and I got distracted re-reading passages I had enjoyed. At last, the books were all tucked away—out of sight but within easy reach. I took a break, sat back in my golden wicker chair, looked at my handiwork, and congratulated myself. Taking breaks seemed to be an imperative part of clearing space.

Next, I tackled the piles of papers, notes, and the many

pictures, art objects, and just plain *stuff* that covered every surface—tables, floor, chairs, and shelves—of the room. I filed away notes and papers and tucked tchotchkes, pictures, and other distracting items into faraway bookshelves or drawers. As the surfaces began to clear, I had a shot of satisfaction. I was enjoying this process. Minimalizing, I called it—making the room feel simplified, clean, open.

It was time for another break. It was long past lunchtime. I trotted down to the kitchen to help myself to an arugula and pinenut salad and fifteen minutes of MSNBC. I further congratulated myself on my progress by having a glass of wine. Refreshed and ready to rejoin the battle with my stuff, I trotted back to the study, ready for more putting away.

The final step of this purgative minimalizing was to clear my desk. I had put this task off until last as I knew it would be the hardest. I have a wide desk that runs the length of the western end of my study, fronted by a large, eight-pane window that looks out on the neighboring yards, rooftops, and distant clouds that turn a hazy purple and orange in the winter sunsets.

The surface of the desk on this day held four different stacks of books, notebooks, files, a large computer monitor, modem and plug-in outlets, cards with jottings or quotes I liked, an open At-A-Glance paper calendar, a radio, recent letters, bills and other communications, rocks from Maine used as paperweights, and multiple to-do lists on colored index cards spread out for optimal visibility. I always enjoyed looking at my piles—like old friends, they keep me company when I am at my desk, distracting me from whatever I am doing. But now I was banishing distractions. It was time to put all of this away—out of sight. Again I set about it and, like a mind sweeper, summarily swept all of these items into drawers and shelves.

It was miraculous, the difference it made. Once cleared, my desk looked like an airport tarmac—open and ready for take-offs. I had a sudden sense of possibility. I was sure, if I just sat down at my newly cleared desk, in an analogous process, my head would clear, and I would be able to give myself over to whatever was going to happen.

That night, when my husband got home, he strolled down the hall toward my study, already talking (as much to himself as to me as I couldn't hear him very well when he was at the end of the hall) about something that had happened that day at work. But he stopped abruptly as he entered my study ... seemingly awed by the disappearance of the usual piles of papers, pictures, books, tchotchkes, and general clutter that usually filled up the available spaces in the room.

"What's going on?" he asked. He was always a bit suspicious whenever I rearranged things—like furniture or clutter or the food in the refrigerator. He felt rearrangement to be a harbinger of changes to come, and he liked to be forewarned. And, let's be frank, I had made some significant personal and professional 'rearrangements' in the last couple of years.

"I am becoming a writer," I said. "This is the first step. Clearing the decks."

"And what are you going to write about?" he asked.

"I haven't the slightest idea," I said. "And until I can figure that out, I am approaching this as if I were starting a meditation practice. Don't all those meditators talk about 'emptying' the mind, clearing out the distractions, and devoting time and space to being open to whatever arrives in your head? So I am practicing emptying and clearing—literally and figuratively. Brilliant, right?"

"Absolutely brilliant," he said with that small smile he uses when humoring me. "I can't wait to see what happens." He settled into the wicker chair and went back to talking about his day at work.

He knew this was new territory for me and that I really didn't know what would happen or if anything would come of this. But I had to hand it to him ... he didn't question or doubt the effort.

It turned out that, for many months, my new writing practice consisted of a great deal of time spent sitting at that desk and looking out the window. I watched and waited. I stared at the Ethiopian Embassy roof next door. I stared at the bare branches of winter trees. I gazed at the slowly fading purple-to-pink-to-light-salmon colors of the disappearing sun. I was "waiting for the aquarium to settle so that ... (I could) see the fish," as memoirist Abigail Thomas describes this part of the writing process.

Often at sunset, I would watch a flock of pointy-winged swallows wheel and dive through the air above the roof. All at once, they'd drop out of the sky and settle into the leafless sycamore tree opposite my window. Small, winging objects perfectly aligned, carving patterns against the darkening blue-black sky.

If I hadn't been staring out the window so frequently, I would have missed these mesmerizing flockings. They mirrored the dipping and darting of my thoughts as I sat hour after hour trying to figure out what I was thinking and then write about it. This kind of thinking was very different from what I was used to. It required patience and a determination not to jump to familiar conclusions. It meant going beyond what I'd understood in the past to be true and being open to wherever my darting thoughts led me. So, when I sat down at my desk to visit my writing each day, as advised by my writing coach, I willed myself to give up wanting a sense of destination or direction and to just go with the flow of my cavorting mind.

For a long while, nothing particularly coherent emerged in my daily writing. Instead, I felt like a collector of artifacts. Each morning, in between trips to the kitchen to refuel on my ink-black coffee, I would sit down at my desk and write whatever arrived in my head: dreams, images, memories, reflections on myself, my family, the world, life, questions, stories I had heard or read about. One day I wrote about the dream I had had the night before: a weathered old woman wearing a deep blue, velvet sweater walked toward me down a long empty beach. When she came close, she peered up at me and then, in a hurried whisper, said, "Olivia has dreamt her way into a new future." *Was Olivia my newly evolving alter ego; the new me?*

Another day I just jotted down fragments of memories of growing up in Michigan—the sunlit smell of freshly mown grass in the spring outside my second-grade school window; the odd, crackling noise of fishflies lying in the road being run over by our car; the taste of maple syrup and hot melted butter that smothered the fat pancakes we gobbled before church every Sunday morning; the sharp, tangy cold of winter mornings as we hurried out the door and piled into the powder blue Morris Minor my mother drove on the way to school; the sleety, leaden days of

February when it felt like the sun would never return.

This led me to ponder and write about the experience of growing up in a deeply-conservative, all-white suburb with parents who were outspoken Democrats and worked in downtown Detroit. Was this why I so often preferred an outlier stance vis-a-vis any group I chose to join? I had been an odd duck in my hometown. Did this affect how I thought about things today? In fact, in a revelationary burst, I had to ask myself—was being retired just another version of being an outlier? Was this new slant on my retired status yet another way I would re-define myself at this stage of my life? Grist for my newly emerging mill of re-invention?

When I couldn't think of anything to write, I would list peculiar words I had come across that tickled my fancy and fired up my imagination— like hummadruz (a low, unexplained humming sound), or ludic (showing spontaneous and undirected playfulness), or flahoolick (open-handed, generous, expansive), or inchoate (just begun and so not fully formed or developed), or lagom (a Swedish word for not too little and not too much).

I became intrigued with small, idiosyncratic details, random facts or ideas or things observed that didn't fit the norm, that surprised or perplexed me and that might require more research: dragonflies have large compound eyes (bifocal vision) that allow them to see in every direction; Finland is purported to have the world's best educational system; the migrating sandpipers we see feeding on the beach in Maine were getting ready to fly two thousand miles to South America for the winter; Matisse, at age 71, called his cut-outs process "painting with scissors" and only began this when he could no longer paint.

This kind of meandering thinking with no explicit goal was, for me, a form of waking woolgathering, psychic romping, a momentary escape from troubling current events—a flight into the world of reverie, play, imaginative delirium. George Sanders, in an interview about writing, describes such mental hijinks as "the artistic uncoupling from the actual." To me it felt like being on a Tilt-a-Whirl ride at the carnival I used to go to every June when I was a kid—jumpily unsettling and intoxicating at the same time, throwing me in one direction and then another, fast and faster ... until we slowed to a stop. That ride rearranged me. I always walked away a bit dizzy—tossled, jostled but undaunted and freshly alive in the moment, wanting more of that kind of adventure. Now I felt similarly rearranged by my mental expeditions. After a morning of writing attempts, I would come away dizzy, jostled but intoxicated by looking at things in my life from new angles, upside down and slanted, in a search for different under-standings, new truths.

I questioned and wondered a lot. WHY? HOW COME? WHAT? and even WHAT IF? I'd decided basic assumptions were no longer inviolable. It became natural to challenge the way I used to think with questions such as:

What does it mean to be happy in a world so grim?
How was it that I could feel such a sense of peace and even a growing mischievous pleasure as I became more and more comfortable with my retired life when wars, injustice, poverty, cataclysmic climate events, and other chaotic and catastrophic situations were happening all around the world? Despite all of the world's chaos, sitting

at my desk trying to write, I experienced moments of hilarity accompanied by a kind of bubbling excitement and pure gratitude. I felt free from responsibility. At the same time, I knew how vastly lucky I was to be so free and at times struggled with the incongruity of being thus when so many were not.

Why do I have to believe what experts tell us? Was I at a point in my life where I had enough information, experience, and even wisdom to challenge what the experts told us? Could I arrive at different conclusions from the pundits based on what I knew and thought? For example—did I have to buy into the negative narrative about being inevitably *aged* and much diminished once I had turned 60, or could a new chapter of life begin at this stage like the authors I had been reading suggested? For me, right then, being *aged* (60 and beyond) felt more like being ripened and ready—seasoned for new experiences and ventures. Maybe this was what Catherine Bateson had meant when she spoke of the achievement of 'active wisdom' at this new stage of later life.

How is it that what I want and do now is so different than what it used to be? For all of my adult life, I'd been extroverted, and the majority of my days were spent in interactions with people. And I'd been a linear thinker—focused on an end goal and systematically following concrete steps to try to achieve what I set out to do. Now I was more introverted, less goal-oriented, more playful, experimenting while improvising a new way of being and thinking. For whatever reason, what I wanted to do and be now was no longer the same as it had been in the past.

I didn't have answers to these questions or others I began to ask, and maybe never would have clear answers, but that didn't worry me. The more I stayed with this process, the more I dared to have faith that whatever it was that was emerging from this untidy, spiraling, open-ended exploration would eventually make some sense to me and be worth trying to translate and write about. I came to see it as what Dani Shapiro, the author of *Still Writing,* has described as a process of "dismantling my ordinary" in the service of discovering the out of ordinary that lay behind or beyond it.

Finally, after months of watching, waiting, and then writing, I began to recognize and understand the story I was trying to tell and why I needed to tell it. The pieces began to fall into place. Over the last few years, I had let go of so much—a career, a family house, my duties and role as a parent to unmarried children, a working identity, familiar routines and habits, and myriad ways I had recognized myself in the past. I had *retired* from so many things. I had 'dismantled' my old life and was in the midst of reassembling a new life that I was finding invigoratingly different. I couldn't have been more surprised and pleased with the changes that I might in the past have dreaded.

I was once a woman who woke up earlier than I wanted to every morning. I was in motion and out the door—busy, scheduled, sociable—dressed in jackets and boots for work, not play. I was involved with people and projects. I spent much of my time interacting with people—clients, colleagues, students, supervisors, friends, and family members, including my children and husband. I was seldom alone, had little time to be still and reflective.

In my new 'retired' life, I was alone a lot. In fact, I was

spending immense amounts of time at home, keeping company with myself, much of the time at my desk. Most mornings, instead of heading out the door, I would sit down at my desk, fire up my computer, and wait to see what would happen. Hours opened out in front of me, forcing me to stay still and open to what might appear there, for me to begin to make sense of and write about. Alert, watching, and waiting, I was a Venus flytrap waiting to capture the passing glittering fly, the prize. I had gone from being very much in the marketplace of a busy life, in conversation with many, to being monkishly at home, away from daily events and conversations, alone with myself. And, as the saying goes, I was "happy as a clam at high tide" having the freedom to spend my days like this.

Retiring, for me, was perhaps one of the riskiest things I had done in my life—a swan dive into deeply unknown territory. It had also shocked me by being one of the most creative and enlivening steps I had ever taken. The freedom to immerse myself in imaginative explorations, to spend time simply being curious and following random thoughts wherever they would lead me in writing, what a nourishing boon to my life this had been. At the same time, it had forced me to grow new muscles, to find entirely new ways of relating to a world and a daily experience that was so different from the ones of my past.

One day, sitting at my desk and once again staring out the window at the bare, black, spindly branches of winter trees, it came to me, clear as a bell ringing in the silence of a dark night. Writing about my journey—from a working life through retirement and beyond—had been my way of meeting myself anew. This is the story I was now determined to tell: my own story about retirement and re-wirement. I was writing as a way to look and look again at my life—digging for the truth of how all this change, all this newness I felt in myself, had come to be. And to find out how I'd gotten to where I had arrived.

I never imagined my explorations in writing would become a book ... not ever. So this memoir is one of those unimagined outcomes—the something that arrives unexpectedly—the unthought-of possibility.

Chapter Eleven
Summing Up

It is the third day of January 2020 as I set out to write this last chapter. That seems significant—a new year, a new decade beginning—even as I use this time to reflect on the last decade, a decade full of change for me. A time that has been bewildering, frightening, exhilarating, demanding, liberating, titillating, and finally, truly gratifying.

Eight years after I closed the door of my office and said goodbye to my clients, here I am. I don't resemble the self I thought I knew. My life doesn't resemble the life I used to have. And retirement (and being over 60) has certainly not been anything I might have expected. Instead, it has been an unanticipated new chapter of my life ... a new-found land where there have been many new and old ideas and assumptions to re-think, re-evaluate, and integrate. It has been a process for me of what Mark Epstein, a Buddhist psychiatrist, describes as an "experience of simultaneously forgetting and discovering oneself." Without totally understanding what I have been doing in these years since retiring, I have systematically revisited how I thought about many things—sifting, sorting, figuring out what no longer fits in my life now. And I couldn't have done this if I hadn't set myself free.

I am clearly not done retiring or re-wiring or, for that matter, evolving into this new chapter as yet. But, as I bumble along, I continue to be awed by what this freedom can offer.

What *does* this freedom offer—beyond the reduction of demands, stress, responsibility, and the need to perform and to prove myself in the working world? Simply said, with so fewer obligations, this freedom invites me to *be*, not *do* ... to experience the world moment to moment, to quiet down and think more slowly, to listen more closely to what comes up from inside rather than react to external chatter and stimulation. Somewhere along the line, I came upon the Elizabeth Gilbert quote: "Sit quietly and cease your relentless participation." This is exactly what I needed to do. I needed and wanted to become a watcher, an observer, to notice what I may have missed in my busy externally-oriented life; to go deeper, to open out to what I had yet to imagine or discover. And being free has allowed this to happen.

This freedom has also given me the space, time, and creative impetus to write and to use the writing practice as my way of making sense of all of this. I will continue to write to better understand who I am now, where I came from, what I think about it, and other things that catch my attention or puzzle or trouble me.

In his 2013 book *The Wonder of Aging*, Michael Gurian urges us older folk to "consider becoming more visible as you age. Find your voice as an aging person and give that voice to the world. Become a game-changer in your home, neighborhood, community, and culture. Go inward when you must, and return outward with art and life that others can see and learn from. Be the 'wise one,' the 'sage,' the 'teacher.' The world needs you as a person over 50 to guide and shape it."

Now that I am way past 50, even way past 60, I realize I have followed his advice. By writing about myself and my bumbling journey into retirement and beyond, I have—reluctantly but steadfastly—become more visible, both to myself and hopefully to others. I write about this to bring it all into the light of day, not just for my own sake but for anyone who might be interested and want to reflect on what all the changes of the later years—the letting go, retirement, potential rewirement, and the newly discovered freedom—might hold. Given what I have found in my retirement, I want to encourage others to take the leap, to vault themselves into the next chapter, to consider what life might hold for them after they get done doing what they used to do.

As some wise person (I can't remember who) advised when looking ahead into this particular future, when you feel ready to retire, *"resist normal impulses and cultivate unimagined possibility."*

Books That Shaped My Thinking
for this Memoir

Bridges, William. *Transitions: Making Sense of Life's Changes*. Reading, MA: Addison-Wesley Publish. 2nd Edition, 2004.

William Bridges is an author, organizational consultant, and a developmental thinker. He defines transition as the "psychological adaptation to change," a process of inner re-orientation and self re-definition crucial to the integration of change that is happening externally. His Transition Model is comprised of three stages: Endings, Neutral Zone, and New Beginnings. This developmental template shaped my understanding of the process of retirement. Embedded in such thinking is that there is, of necessity, a "gap between one life phase and another," a limbo—empty time where one can "cultivate receptivity" to what unfamiliar possibilities the future may hold. His writing is both philosophical and down-to-earth. He cites Greek myth, multiple cultural traditions, and modern psychological theory as well as very human examples of transitions many people undergo.

Cohen, Gene. *The Creative Age: Awakening Human Potential in the Second Half of Life*. New York: Avon Books, 2000.

Gene Cohen has been called 'the guru' of the potential for creativity in the second half of life. In this book, he not only debunks myths about inevitable declines in older people but also explains in lay terms biological brain function and creative potential as we age. The book is replete with inspiring examples of what people have accomplished later in life. Robert Frost at age 87 wrote *The Gift Outright* and read it at President Kennedy's inauguration; Katherine Graham at age 79 wrote her first book *Personal History*, which won a Pulitzer Prize. Also included are many salient and thought-provoking quotes: "Discovery consists of looking at the same thing as everyone else and thinking something different." – Albert Szent-Gyorgyi. "A living thing is distinguished from a dead thing by the multiplicity of changes at any moment taking place in it." – Herbert Spenser, biologist. In several Appendices, he offers concrete recommendations about aging well including a step-by-step technique for creating an autobiography and multiple internet and other resources.

Levine, Suzanne Braun. *Inventing the Rest of Our Lives: Women in Second Adulthood*. New York: Penguin Group, 2005.

Suzanne Braun Levine is an author of many books and one of the early editors of Ms. Magazine. Her writing focuses on the evolution and empowerment of women after the age of 50. This time of life, which she calls Second Adulthood, offers us an "unprecedented and productive time" in which there is the opportunity—if not the imperative—for women to shed outgrown roles and to take time to 'recalibrate.' It is a time to ask ourselves "what matters, what works, and what's next?" in different ways than we have before. Questions such as these, she says, lead to the possibility of unanticipated reinventions. She offers research, theory, advice, personal stories, and many examples of women and herself upending outdated ways of thinking about themselves and reimagining their futures. She balances this positive narrative with discussions of the real issues facing women as they let go of old roles and work to find new ways of coping with life after 50.

Sadler, William & Krefft, James. *Changing Course: Navigating Life after Fifty.* Centennial, Co: The Center for Third Age Leadership Press, 2007.

Sadler, William. *The Third Age: Six Principles of Growth and Renewal After Forty.* Cambridge, Massachusetts: Perseus Publishing, 2000.

William Sadler, a sociologist, spent years researching "alternative models of midlife and aging" and concluded that prevailing negative aging paradigms were out-of-date. Instead, he challenges us to look at the second half of our lives (our 'Third Age') as a time of renewal and new growth—an opportunity to create an entirely new life design. The book includes his Six Principles of Growth and Renewal—specific suggestions as to how to re-design your life: mindfulness and risk-taking, realistic optimism, a positive third age identity, balancing work and play, personal freedom and intimacy, and building a more caring life. Each chapter is fleshed out with examples from interviews with people between the ages of 40 and 80.

Walton, Mark. *Boundless Potential: Transform Your Brain, Unleash Your Talents, Reinvent Your Work in Midlife and Beyond*. New York: McGraw Hill Companies, 2012.

Walton's book—filled as it is with stories about real people, later in life, reinventing themselves—is thoroughly inspiring. Older adults are "hardwired for reinvention," he argues, and there is neuroscientific research done in the last twenty years that proves it. He exhorts people to think differently about this stage of life: to challenge ourselves and branch out, to continue to grow in ways hitherto unexplored, and to develop entirely new skills and interests that take us in directions we may have never gone. Best of all, he includes concrete suggestions and methods for "realizing" this new potential and finding new meaning and purpose in our later lives.

Other Good Books About Life in the Second Half

Alboher, Marci. *The Encore Career Workbook.* New York: Workman Publishing, 2013.

Bateson, Catherine. *Composing a Further Life: The Age Of Active Wisdom.* New York: Random House, 2010.

Cohen, Gene. *The Mature Mind: The Positive Power of the Aging Brain.* Cambridge, MA: Basic Books, 2005.

Corbett, David with Higgins, Richard. *Portfolio Life.* San Francisco, CA: John Wiley & Sons, 2007.

Csikszentmihalyi, Mihaly. *Flow: The Psychology of Optimal Experience.* New York: Harper Perennial Modern Classics, 1990.

De Hennezel, Marie. *The Warmth of the Heart Prevents Your Body From Rusting.* England: London: Rodale Press, 2011.

Dychtwald , Ken and Kadlec, Daniel. *The Power Years: A User's Guide to the Rest of Your Life.* Hoboken, NJ: Wiley, 2005.

Frankel, Bruce. *What Should I Do With the Rest of MY Life: True Stories of Finding Success, Passion and New Meaning in the Second Half of Life.* Penguin Group, 2010.

Freedman, Marc. *Encore: Finding Work that Matters in the Second Half of Life.* New York: PublicAffairs, 2007.

Freedman, Marc. *The Big Shift: Navigating The New Stage Beyond Midlife.* New York: PublicAffairs Books, 2011.

Gurian, Michael. *The Wonder of Aging.* New York: Atria Books, 2013.

Hall, Stephen. *Wisdom: From Philosophy to Neuroscience.* 2010.

Lawrence-Lightfoot, Sara. *The Third Chapter.* New York: Sarah Crichton Books, 2009.

Nuland, Shep. *Art Of Aging.* New York, NY: Random House, 2007.

Roosevelt, Eleanor. *You Learn By Living.* New York: Harper Perennial, 1960.

Sellars, Jeri & Miners, Rick. *Don't Retire, Rewire!* New York: Penguin Books, 2007.

Strauch, Barabara. *The Secret Life of the Grown Up Brain.* New York: Penguin Books, 2010.

The Transition Network and Rentsch, Gail. *Smart Women Don't Retire – They Break Free.* New York: Springboard Press, 2008.

Valliant, George. *Aging Well*. Boston, MA: Little Brown and Company, 2002.

Other Reading

Epstein, Mark. *Going to Pieces Without Falling Apart.* New York: Broadway Books, 1998.

Johnson, Charles Murray. *The Creative Imperative.* Berkley, California: Celestial Arts, 1986.

Pipher, Mary. *Writing to Change The World*. Berkley, California: Berkley Publishing Group, 2006.

Shapiro, Dani. *Still Writing*. New York: Grove Press, 2013.

Thomas, Abigail. *Thinking About Memoir*. New York: Sterling Publishing, 2008.

Acknowledgments

First and foremost, I want to thank my writing 'coach' and mentor—Sara Taber—whose encouragement and endless support pushed me to make my rambling musings about retirement and being 'older' grow and coalesce into something I had never imagined—a book. Writing this memoir—with her help and enlightened guidance—gave me the chance to make sense of the journey and see my way beyond and forward. I will always be grateful.

Along the way I have talked to countless people who have generously shared their own insights and perspectives on retirement, on possibility, opportunity, and reinventions in the Third Age and about life in general: Adele D'Ari, Ted Coates, Stacey Coates, Susan Drobis, Tim Garrity, Joan and Michael Goldfrank, Davye Gould, Sandra Horowitz, Kirk Markwald, Susan Mikesell, Wendy Miller, Stephen Milliken, Truman Morrison, Judy Perkins, Catherine Pierce, Brian Schwartz, Patsy Taylor and Chris Whipple, among others. In particular, I want to thank Susan Mikesell for all the time and thinking she did with me during this time. She and I have had monthly conversations for the last six years, reviewing the research and literature about transition and potential in later life and reflecting on what we both were discovering about retirement and what might come after. She has been instrumental in helping me gain a new perspective on creativity and aging, while sharing her very unique insights and personal wisdom and epiphanies.

I am deeply grateful for the patience and generosity of all the people I interviewed for this memoir: Nancy Carson, Jeff Drobis, Susan Flanders, Joan Goldfrank,

Elisabeth Hazard, Desiree Magney, Jeff Mayer, Tina and David Mead, Roger Pasquier, Sule Patek, Kathy Swartz, Linda Turner, John Wimberly, and all the members of my book group. They not only agreed to be interviewed and perhaps included in my book, but also patiently put up with my sometimes nonsensical questions.

These conversations and interviews have been an indispensable ingredient in the making of this memoir. My life has been enriched by each and every one of them.

Finally, I want to thank my husband for his good humor, forbearance, and great ideas.

I am particularly grateful that he didn't mind terribly when I told stories about him.

About the Author

Rebecca Milliken enjoyed a forty-year career as a teacher, arts therapist, licensed professional counselor, and clinical researcher and writer in Washington D.C. In 2012, Rebecca took a leap and closed her clinical practice without knowing what would come next. Since then, she has devoted herself to exploring the possibilities that life offers in retirement. She has written a memoir about her own transition from a long career to an invigorating, reconfigured life of newfound passions. Inspired by her research and her own experience, she wants to encourage others to embrace rather than dread this time of life.

About Atmosphere Press

Atmosphere Press is an independent, full-service publisher for excellent books in all genres and for all audiences. Learn more about what we do at atmospherepress.com.

We encourage you to check out some of Atmosphere's latest releases, which are available at Amazon.com and via order from your local bookstore:

Convergence: The Interconnection of Extraordinary Experiences, a book by Barbara Mango and Lynn Miller

Sacred Fool, a biography by Nathan Dean Talamantez

My Place in the Spiral, a photographic memoir by Rebecca Beardsall

My Eight Dads, a memoir by Mark Kirby

Vespers' Lament, essays by Brian Howard Luce

Without Her: Memoir of a Family, by Patsy Creed

One Warrior to Another, a memoir by Richard Cleaves

Emotional Liberation: Life Beyond Triggers and Trauma, nonfiction by GuruMeher Khalsa

The Space Between Seconds, a book by NY Haynes

License to Learn, a book by Anna Switzer, PhD

The Bond, a memoir by A. M. Grotticelli

Sex—Interrupted: Igniting Intimacy While Living With Illness or Disability, a book by Iris Zink and Jenny Palter

Between Each Step: A Married Couple's Thru Hike On New Zealand's Te Araroa, a memoir by Patrice LaVigne